ST. FRANCIS OF ASSISI

ALSO BY JON M. SWEENEY

A Course in Christian Mysticism, by Thomas Merton (editor)

The Enthusiast: How the Best Friend of Francis of Assisi Almost Destroyed What He Started

Francis of Assisi in His Own Words: The Essential Writings, 2nd ed. (translator and editor)

Inventing Hell: Dante, the Bible, and Eternal Torment, Second Edition, foreword by Richard Rohr

Meister Eckhart's Book of the Heart: Meditations for the Restless Soul (with Mark S. Burrows)

The Pope Who Quit: A True Medieval Tale of Mystery, Death, and Salvation

The Road to Assisi: The Essential Biography of St. Francis, by Paul Sabatier (editor)

The St. Clare Prayer Book: Listening for God's Leading

The St. Francis Prayer Book: A Guide to Deepen Your Spiritual Life

When Saint Francis Saved the Church: How a Converted Medieval Troubadour Created a Spiritual Vision for the Ages

ST. FRANCIS OF ASSISI

His Life, Teachings, and Practice

ESSENTIAL WISDOM LIBRARY

Jon M. Sweeney

ST. MARTIN'S
ESSENTIALS
New York

First published in the United States by St. Martin's Essentials,
an imprint of St. Martin's Publishing Group

For information, address St. Martin's Publishing Group,
120 Broadway, New York, NY 10271.

www.stmartins.com

All translations of the words of St. Francis of Assisi are the author's renderings into a twenty-first-century English idiom. All quotations from the Bible are from the New Revised Standard Version (NRSV), Catholic Edition, used with permission.

The Library of Congress Cataloging-in-Publication Data is available upon request.

ISBN 978-1-250-20965-8 (trade paperback)
ISBN 978-1-250-20966-5 (ebook)

First Edition: October 2019

10 9 8 7 6 5 4 3 2 1

For Adam

Contents

Foreword by Richard Rohr, O.F.M. *ix*

Chronology *xiii*

INTRODUCTION 1

St. Francis Changed My Life 7

Some Quick History 16

What Francis Accomplished 22

FRANCIS'S TEACHINGS 37

FRANCIS'S SPIRITUAL PRACTICES 90

Seeking the Vulnerable 95

Blessing Animals, Stones, Fish, Sun, and Moon 97

Holy Foolishness 98

Denial and Dance 99

Finding Joy 101

FINAL THOUGHTS 103

Notes *105*

If You Want to Read More *107*

Acknowledgments *110*

About the Author *111*

Foreword

The trouble with being an "official," habit-wearing Franciscan, and one who has written or talked about St. Francis so many times myself, is that I fear I have become jaded with his very beauty, and in my later years even mistrustful of my lifetime fascination with this man, whose vision has framed my whole life and yet left me in the dust. I am almost afraid to be infatuated again. I read such books as this with immense hesitation.

Here we have yet another book on Francis (is this what we really need?) and it is now in your hands, as it has just been in mine. I must be honest and admit that if it were not for my trust and friendship with Jon Sweeney, I would never have agreed to write these few words in what I hope can be a sincere invitation and positive gateway to the whole book.

But now I am glad that I did agree. This seems to be the way that God always works—at least with me—always ambushing us while we are on the road to somewhere else. That has been the major story line of my whole life, and I think of Francis's life, too. Maybe it is even the most normal path. Who of us could or would effectively steer the boat of our own transformation? God has become expert at the art of ambush.

Of the many memorable reflections and quotes in this book, there is one that haunted me in the introduction itself:

Most of us "decide to remain essentially who we are, now, except that who we are now is mostly who we have been, and who we have been began in us when we were children." Most of us are on autopilot, determined by the urgent context of our life at every stage.

My God, that is true for most humans I have ever met, including myself! It shows me how rare true conversion really is, and how once you allow this process—there is really no stopping it. Although we surely try. Still, you are hooked! Because there is really nothing better than divine love once you have tasted it.

Once the divine ambush is first allowed it seems to continue unabated through one's whole life. In time, you begin to recognize the signs, and one of the first is a strange kind of *resistance*—from nowhere in particular. (Although you add your rationalizations.) Once you are hooked, you feel like saying with Jeremiah the prophet "You have seduced me, God, and I have let myself be seduced . . . I say to myself 'I will not think about you anymore, until there seems to be a fire burning in my heart'" (Jeremiah 20:7,9). And the tug-of-war and love begins all over again.

I agree wholeheartedly with Jon's assertion that both Francis and Clare saw their lives (which they state explicitly in their

Rules) as a way of life, or *forma vitae,* as opposed to a doctrinal or ecclesiastical career. Today we would call it orthopraxy over any major arguments about verbal orthodoxy. We were balanced out nicely in that regard by our companions, the Order of Preachers, or the Dominicans. We mostly left the academics to them, probably selfishly or lazily on our part, but it freed us for another vocation—lifestyle itself. Not what you think, but how you act. Some now call it "performative Christianity" and we find it continuously rediscovered by groups as varied as the Waldensians, the Beguines, the Mennonites, the Amish, the Little Brothers and Sisters of Jesus, Twelve Step spirituality, and the Catholic Workers today.

Ironically, *doers* always look "lightweight," exactly as many fearful people consider Pope Francis today. Is this not what St. Paul, St. Francis, and Jon Sweeney call "Holy Foolishness"? "God showed me how to work with my hands," he says in his final *Testament.* It is really quite amazing, isn't it, that doing is considered less important than thinking? Action less needed than believing things correctly? I am not sure that this clerical imbalance has much to show for itself today in the many countries that were once fully Christian and are now mostly secular or communist.

Jon ends his book with a wonderful translation of Francis's own description of his own conversion as always "turning around" and seeing through and beyond "how everybody thinks and sees" in the dominant consciousness. *Francis did not think himself into a new way of living, but he lived himself into a new way of thinking,* beginning with his "living among the lepers" and putting in our very title that we were all to be "Brothers of the Lower Class" (*Frati Minori*). It was not merely a change of ideas, but a change of class and perspective. A movement from the side of privilege and power to the side of powerlessness, which addicts call the very First Step—"to admit that you are powerless."

So be scandalized, infatuated, shamed, and in-spirited once again that our faith and love is so feeble compared to this *vir catholicus* (antiphon for the feast of St. Francis), this "truly universal man" who seems to have the job of nudging all of history out of its too-easy complacency, and inviting Christianity into that one and unique love affair with both God and with the whole world at the same time. Francis showed us they were one and the same love. In fact, the official motto of the Friars Minor to this day is *Deus Meus et Omnia*, correctly translated as "My God—and all things."

Richard Rohr, O.F.M
Center for Action and Contemplation
Albuquerque, New Mexico

Chronology

Many of these dates are approximate. Precise records were rarely kept.

1181 (the second half of the year). Born Giovanni di Pietro di Bernardone. His father calls him Francesco, "Francis."

1202 (fall). Francis spends time in prison in Perugia, captive in a skirmish between Perugia and Assisi.

1205 (spring). Francis leaves again for war but returns home the following day.

1205 (mid-year). He is first sickened, then graced, by lepers. "God led me among them," Francis later says. (Later that year), Francis hears the voice of God while kneeling in prayer in the church of San Damiano.

1206 (spring). Francis and his father separate in front of the bishop and the town of Assisi.

1208 (spring). Francis moves from simply rebuilding churches to preaching and caring for the sick.

1208 (April 16). Two men, Bernard and Peter, become Francis's first companions. A companion must get rid of all possessions. Sometime later that year they begin to live in and around a little chapel, called Portiuncula, in the valley below Assisi.

1209 (spring). Now twelve in number, Francis and his companions walk to Rome to see the pope.

1217–18 The mission expands. Francis sends friars to Africa, the Middle East, and parts of Eastern and Western Europe.

1219 Francis travels to meet the sultan in the Nile Delta while the Fifth Crusade is ongoing.

1220 Francis steps down from leadership of the religious order, appointing a vicar-general from among the other friars.

1225 (spring). Ill and dying, staying near St. Clare at San Damiano, Francis composes a joyful celebration of creation, "Canticle of the Creatures."

1226 (October 3). Dying, Francis asks the friars to take him to Portiuncula. He dies that evening.

1228 (July 16). St. Francis is canonized by Pope Gregory IX. Before his election as pope, Gregory IX had been the cardinal responsible for oversight of the Franciscans.

What would you do today if you knew
you might die tomorrow?

—ST. FRANCIS

Introduction

To grasp St. Francis of Assisi's spirit is to be liberated. A person can experience it right where they live by embracing the freedom, vulnerability, foolishness, and gentleness that Francis lived and taught. I see this happen when people begin to catch these aspects of his life and pull them into their own lives for the first time—replacing egoism, illusion, and fear.

Such freedom can, however, be disruptive. Relationships that are not life-giving can become obvious, when before they were easily accommodated. Work that doesn't feed the soul begins to feel increasingly intolerable. Time spent is evaluated differently, especially if one's common use of free time is revealed to be captive to what no longer really matters.

People can experience St. Francis on a more metaphysical level, as well, as a liberation of the energies that are properly and naturally stored inside them. There are energies inside us that have become cramped and distorted over the years—the result of many negative experiences in our past and present. These gather in and around our stress, responsibilities, and relationships. This is when life feels like it's going nowhere or is stalled or we simply can't seem to break through to something richer, better, or vital. Our energies, created for our well-being, are finding no adequate channel for their true activity, for the true activity of the energies inside us—what Christians call the Holy Spirit—is satisfying and sweet. We are meant to be inspired, creative, supportive, optimistic people. If our lives don't feel this sweetness, we need liberation. Francis showed long ago with his life and teachings how to go about this.

An analogy helps: Our bodies and spirits are like electric batteries. The mysterious power they contain is latent, just waiting for a switch to be flipped so that a current can move. What it takes to flip that switch can vary a great deal from one person to the next. For some of us it takes more of a jolt than it does for others. Perhaps it's like the live wires we sometimes connect between a running engine and a dead engine in an effort to bring the dead one back to life. If you are such a person, requiring such a jolt, you have something in common with Francis as he entered adult life.

Soon, when we turn to the key moments in Francis's life, you may conclude that he was overly dramatic. This may be true, but it only tells part of the story. Francis used gestures to communicate, and shows of emotion before others, all in the service of his conversion. This is because sometimes he was doing what he had to do—shocking himself to life, almost like one would jump-start that battery that's dead—to liberate himself from what keeps people living without life. In other words, he seems to have known that he had to sometimes be dramatic.

He wasn't alone in his era as a religious person of dramatic gestures and intensely expressed emotions. The early thirteenth century was marked by many—for example, lay religious women called Beguines. They were lay religious, not nuns. They lived semi-monastically and were known for having the "gift of tears" and seeking forms of public humiliation to express their devotion to God. They were more independent than nuns were, but they were religiously intense. These Beguines were sometimes known by other, even more exotic names, such as tertiaries, *klopjes,* recluses, and anchoresses. But exoticism aside, this was a time when it became common for ordinary people to be personally convicted of something spiritually lacking in life and then go about fixing it in public. Francis's half century, it could be said, witnessed the birth of demonstrative Christian mysticism.[1] This can feel strange to us today, but it once wasn't.

I think of the medieval Mystery Plays. They were dramatic, public, bloody, loud reenactments of events in the lives of saints or Christ, especially Christ's Passion. No one ever simply read such a play. One watched and heard and felt it on the front edge of the emotions–while standing and shrieking beside one's neighbors. So the mysticism that was being born was not privately experienced in the way we expect mysticism to be today. Even the celebration of the mass was, from its ancient beginnings, meant to be a performance. The word "mystery," in fact, means "religious performance."[2] All of it drew Francis in.

He never became a priest; he didn't want to be ordained beyond that of a deacon. So he never said a mass himself, even though he led others in religious services from early in his conversion. He used his dramatic flair to awaken others. These services must have seemed odd, even a little dangerous, to people familiar only with the traditional ways of church. Francis learned from the entertainers and storytellers who were popular in late medieval Europe, and set out to introduce holy things, but still hold your attention. This is probably why they became so popular so fast: when Francis began leading religious services, they didn't always seem religious. This is how the Nobel Prize–winner Dario Fo puts it:

> Francis would often begin his "services" with dance, transforming his sermon into a kind of musical entertainment, full of lively rhythms, drawing his audience in with stories of love and bawdy passion. Then out of all this earthly carnal love, he would change tack and introduce the purest, most joyful love we owe to our Creator.[3]

He was attempting to open in others those places inside where they had not yet been able to experience God.

Human beings tend toward private expressions of emotion and spirit, and Francis showed a different way, probably a more productive way. The lesson was that no one should be held back by themselves or anyone else when it comes to expressions of life or bringing their spiritual selves back from the dead. The spirit needs to express itself. It needs to be experienced and seen. That can be frightening, when new. Francis showed how to shake off, wake up, turn around, and use your body to stir your soul and the souls of those around you.

When that electric current of ours is stagnant, like the automobile that has sat idle too long in the garage, we grow weak and eventually our battery dies altogether. Imagine turning a key in the ignition and hearing only a sputtering sound, followed by a splat. Francis's spirit saves us from such a fate. His life and teachings are like a jump start for that cold, cold engine. The sputtering doesn't go splat, but the engine begins to roar again, as it was meant to do. This is true freedom: putting to use the creative, inspired, benevolent impulses and energies naturally and supernaturally found within us. Without this freedom to express ourselves, and act, we are lost.

People often fail to notice that they are moving through life aimlessly, like a meteor passing outside the Earth's atmosphere into space.

It can seem, today, that it's impossible to lose our directional way. Every stride has been mapped by someone already. There's no place we can travel that hasn't already been experienced by someone else. The world we see and hear and touch has lost most of its mystery. There is no part that remains unexplored, undocumented, untouched. If you want to see Timbuktu, you watch a video from Timbuktu streamed to the device of your choosing. If you're curious about the turtles of the Galápagos Islands, you find those easily, too. This is our secularism: we've lost the ability to be awed. Presence means nothing.

But there is still God's presence. It is no more clearly mapped, now, than it ever was before. That's not how finding God works.

The other exception is what is obscured from the past. There is no way to re-create the expressions or spirit of people who have gone before us. Study the Oglala Lakota and the history of the Great Plains all you want, but you'll never experience or relive what it was like to encounter a million buffalo in the Black Hills or to be present at an early Ghost Dance. Read all the books about the early Beguines, or the first friends of St. Francis in the valley below Assisi, and you cannot be in that place. We have to accept and approach such mysteries with awe.

So we turn to St. Francis's writings–rules of life, letters to friends and people in power, wishes he had for laypeople and for his friend Clare—and to reliable biographies of what his lifelong conversion was all about. We may not be able to go back in time and re-create that presence, but we do well to learn from what we have. What comes through clearly in Francis's life and teachings are moments when an astonishing union–ecstatic, surrendering, and stunning—takes place with God. This union is the key to everything else. And what happened to him eight hundred years ago still happens in the lives of ordinary people like us.

St. Francis Changed My Life

I was absorbed in myself until I met St. Francis. I was in high school: worried over my appearance, how my hair fell, how to clear up my skin, who liked me, who didn't, where to go on weekends to be around the people I was most impressed with and whom I most wanted to impress. Did I mention I was anxious to have people like me? This is all natural, you might say, and it was. I was typical of others at my age and stage in life, and I was typically lost. I often think it's because of Francis that I didn't become an easily lost adult.

I came across a book one day on a shelf in the public library. I was probably in that deep row of library shelving to hide from someone in the library whom I didn't want to see. What if the wrong person observed me in the library! I noticed this particular book in part because it was the thickest I'd ever seen, and it had a deep cherry-red cover, which was also hard to miss. I pulled it down out of curiosity. *Saint Francis of Assisi: Writings and Early Biographies*. The title page used the phrase "Omnibus of the Sources," and that was interesting. I'd heard of St. Francis. He was the one who liked animals. The book said it was compiled and published by Franciscans, whoever they were.

What's interesting to me now is how my discovery of that book is similar to how people sometimes discovered the Franciscan way of life in Francis's own time. He and the friends who joined in his poor, simple way of living used to introduce strangers to their life similarly to how I became attentive to that conspicuous, unusual book on the shelf. They would send one of their number to a nearby Italian town to see whom they might reach with their Gospel message. He would be dressed strangely, unexpectedly shabby. A friar (that's what they were called—the word means simply "brother") was always dressed shabbily compared to monks, priests, and knights. He would walk, never ride a horse, all the way there. The journey might take days, but if you saw him on the road he wouldn't be asking for a ride. Even in the rain, he'd seem quite happy where he was, doing what he was doing, making his way to wherever he was slowly traveling on foot. He also wouldn't bring food with him but would beg for his bread or hope to find some free fruit on the trees as he walked. He'd sleep under the stars, in a cave, or beneath any temporary shelter. He'd never knock on doors and ask for special treatment. He'd keep mostly to himself, except for singing. Francis and his friends enjoyed making music. All of this was intentional. The rule of life they lived was simple, taken from the Gospels:

> Look at the birds of the air; they neither sow nor reap nor gather into barns, and yet your heavenly Father feeds them. . . . And why do you worry about clothing? Consider the lilies of the field, how they grow; they neither toil nor spin, yet I tell you, even Solomon in all his glory was not clothed like one of these. But if God so clothes the grass of the field, which is alive today and tomorrow is thrown into the oven, will he not much more clothe you—you of little faith? Therefore do not worry, saying, "What will we

> eat?" or "What will we drink?" or "What will we wear?" . . . But strive first for the kingdom of God . . . (Mt. 6:26, 28–31, 33)

By the time this simple friar arrived at his destination, he'd be dusty and hungry. But the Franciscan way was to be joyful in dustiness and hunger. To experience such small hardships was to identify with Christ in his poverty and to thereby partake a little bit of heaven. Christ had divided loaves and fishes to feed large crowds, he had even refused a drink while hanging on the cross, and he'd said not to worry about the needs of tomorrow. So the dusty hungry friar would take a seat in the town square with a grin on his face. I imagine there were exceptions but that most often the grin was genuine joyfulness. The friar had learned how not to worry, how to live in the moment—and for this reason, his look disconcerted ordinary people even more than usual. Inevitably, like that cherry-red book I couldn't help but see on the shelf when I was a nervous teenager, this friar stuck out like a sore thumb.

Very quickly, children would come and mock him. They saw a dirty, shabbily clothed new person in town as a sort of lunatic. Unless you were a young child, life was meant to be a grim matter and a hardworking responsibility. The fact that the friar had what seemed to them to be a silly look on his face made him even more someone to be reviled. He was unfamiliar to them, and children, unless they're taught to appreciate difference, are frightened by unfamiliarity. They also didn't know how else to respond to someone who seemed immune to others' expectations. Some of the adults around the kids were no better.

The mocking—sometimes playful, often less so—might go on for days, until finally someone more sensitive and thoughtful would come sit beside the friar in the piazza and say something like, "Who are you? Why are you here?" It was then that the little poor man (Francis called them Friars Minor, because they deliberately went through life without worldly significance) would pull from the pocket of his tattered cowl a document with some Bible verses on it, shaped just enough to read like a rule of life. Most people knew what *rules* were: written documents of monastic orders, in which the principles for communal life, vows, obedience to an abbot, and so forth, were made clear. Francis's was a bit different, and simpler.

None of the physical copies of this document have survived, which isn't surprising, because they were probably just scraps of paper. It would be a few years before their principles were formed into something worthy of being formally approved by a pope in Rome. When that happened, the language sounded more formal, but certain parts still resembled what a friar would have shared with that first sensitive and thoughtful fellow pilgrim in the town square:

> We should take nothing for ourselves, not a house or any property or things at all. We should remain simple pilgrims and strangers in the world, and serve God in poverty and humility. We should expect nothing, but ask for whatever

> is left over. And we should never be ashamed by this, because our Lord made himself poor in this world. Our hope is in him who can make us heirs of the kingdom of heaven.
>
> Let's treat each other as members of one family, and confidently make known to each other our needs. Consider this: If a mother loves and cherishes the son she raises how much more should we cherish and love one who is our brother according to the Holy Spirit! For example, when one of us falls sick, the others should serve him as they would wish to be served themselves.

That was essentially the cherry-red book I took down that day from the shelf—or, at least, that was the cherry-red book's effect on me.

The first stories of Francis I read were about the friends who deserted him, as well as the friends who joined him in a way of life that was more real than the one he'd previously been trying to live. I realized that Francis, too, was a nervous young man preoccupied with what people thought of him. I read about Francis going off to war when he was not much older than I was. He suited up in the best armor his father could afford, which was a lot, but then soon he was captured. He spent a year in a prison cell in Perugia, a city very near Assisi. Eventually, his father ransomed him and he returned home. Two years later, Francis went to war again, following a famous knight. On the first day of travel, with a destination of Apulia, he only got as far as Spoleto. The following morning, he was perhaps sick. Some of the sources say so; they also sometimes suggest that Francis heard God telling him to return home. Most likely, he came back to Assisi that day in disgrace, as either a deserter or a failure or both. This is the day that his biographers pinpoint as when his conversion began.

I read about Francis's preoccupations with women, wanting to woo them, wanting them to love him, singing to them at night like a sappy troubadour. He seemed to be in love with love, and I felt like I understood that, too. There are scenes, after his return to Assisi from Spoleto, when Francis is out carousing with friends and the friends notice he seems preoccupied. Francis was being visited by God, just then, for the first time, say the authors of *The Legend of the Three Companions*. He was still writing poems to women, which is what I was doing, too. Awful stuff! He was caught up in his passions; he loved how it felt to be filled with such emotion, but somehow it wasn't quite real. He would discover what real love was all about when he finally stopped chasing it.

I read about Francis giving away his possessions, trying to follow the teachings of Jesus in the Gospels in ways that followers of Jesus don't seem to take seriously anymore. Even before his conversion was at full speed, when he was still living at home, he began taking food from his mother's table while his father was out of town and giving it to the poor. A year later, he realized that what God wanted from him was much greater.

No kid who grows up in a comfortable home and reads the New Testament can come away from the experience without thinking, *We don't do what Jesus says, really, at all.* Christians ignore what Jesus said to the first disciples: ". . . If you wish to be perfect, go, sell your possessions, and give the money to the poor, and you will have treasure in heaven; then come, follow me" (Mt. 19:21). This became central to Francis's response to God, too—taking those words seriously. So there was an authenticity about Francis that made immediate sense, not only to my immature self but also to my reflective one.

Then I read about Francis standing up to powerful people on behalf of ordinary people, and traveling to the Nile Delta to see the sultan because he thought there had to be a better option than killing others to make possible safe routes for pilgrims traveling to the Holy Land. It seemed that Francis thought he could end the era of the Crusades simply by meeting with the Muslim sultan. How naïve that made him! It drew me to him even more. The naïveté never went away in Francis, either, something that attracts me to him still. Years after his conversion began, you still see Francis living by those strict Gospel principles. He doesn't grow up and lose all his ideals. You see him still frequently going off by himself, pounding his heart, as if to wake up his soul, or asking no one but God, "Who am I?!"

I'm not courageous. I've never been attracted to martyrdom for my faith. I haven't gone hungry, not really. But the simpler things Francis did I then tried to do. I still try to do them. For example, Francis had problems at home and his relationship with his father was not always good. His dad expected him to become a certain kind of person, one that

Francis didn't want to become. They fought about it. Francis felt that he had, ultimately, to decide if he was going to follow what his father wanted for him or what his conscience—informed by his now intense personal relationship with God—was telling him to do. He chose God. I didn't have such a severe problem with my father as a boy, but since becoming an adult I've believed that every boy must somehow stand up to his father before he can become his own person. Franz Kafka, the Czech fiction writer, once wrote to his dad, saying: "Sometimes I imagine the map of the world spread out and you stretched diagonally across it." Kafka explained that he had to find the places not within his dad's reach, where the young man could come into his own. I think this is what Francis did, and I could relate. Maybe girls are this way with their mothers, too; I wouldn't know.

There was one most important woman in Francis's life, and it wasn't his mother. We know almost nothing about his mom, and he never speaks about her. But you may have heard of St. Clare. She was a friend of Francis and the first woman to join him in what he was doing. She, too, had to separate herself from parental expectations before she could ever become who she was meant to become. It infuriated her family. I was able to relate to all that, and so at times when what seemed right in my life was slightly at odds with what my family of origin thought best I clung closer to Francis–and to Clare.

Even the soldiering spoke to me because I discovered Francis just as I was about to register for Selective Service, as a young man about to turn eighteen. I was supposed to sign up with my government to say, *I'm at your service if necessary to go to war on your behalf and fight and kill for you.* I felt uncomfortable with that. *Doesn't the Gospel teach something else?* Watching Francis's discomfort helped me to discern that registering as a conscientious objector was what was right for me.

Then there were the simple things Francis did or set out to do. When he turned away from what his father expected, he was also turning away from what society expected: householding, family raising, property ownership, respectability, power, and influence as benefiting someone from his sort of background. Francis turning away from these things inspired me, years ago, to de-emphasize them in my life, too. I've had mortgages and raised children. I've never taken a vow of poverty. However, many, many times I have made conscious decisions to go for less, to live more simply, not to seek the job whose primary appeal is the income, to worry less about tomorrow, to do the thing that almost seems contrary to what we're usually taught to do. I've tried to be who God wants me to be, by living according to different principles than those most parents teach their children. I fail all the time. But Francis remains my inspiration. All these principles are as countercultural today as they were in St. Francis's thirteenth century, and for that reason, I think, Francis is the most relevant of Christian saints from centuries ago.

Some Quick History

We usually go through life blind and deaf to what ails us. We tune out most forms of critique and exhortation because it is shrill to hear, and we decide to remain essentially who we are, now, except that who we are is mostly who we have been, and who we have been began in us when we were children. So you can see why most spiritual greats have come to say that we shouldn't sit satisfied in ignorance or laziness—because that's what this often looks, most of all, like in us: ignorance and laziness. There is much more to a happy, productive, blessed life than this. Than what is. Francis realized this, first in his own life. He was given much by his parents and circumstances, but it did not satisfy.

He was a popular boy from a good home. He had everything he needed in terms of security, possessions, and care. He was embraced by many but found that the love he craved was not easy to embrace. With money in his pockets, he was invited to parties and fun to have around. He was a good talker and singer of songs, even late at night under the city windows of girls he desired to woo. He was rarely alone. He was always talking. Until he happened to be without company and everything went quiet and he began to hear something inside of him. What was that sound?

He was graced with charm and personality and enjoyed himself until he glimpsed his vanity. He dreamed of what boys are supposed to dream—for valor and reputation—until he saw his cowardly heart. These were stages of awakening.

God does the awakening in us. We realize and respond to

it. Each stage of awakening in Francis Bernardone was punctuated with dramatic gestures of change. Francis was like the man who realizes that the best way to survive outdoors in the snow and cold underdressed is not to worry or complain or wait for help, but to pick up his footsteps with vigor and yell like a soldier about to charge.

Soon he began to pay attention to small things. This is probably because he was quieting his mind, which opens the imagination and spirit to things previously unnoticed and unseen. If people know Francis today for one thing, it would be his love for creatures: he's the birdbath saint, the one who talked with birds. This is true to who he was, and it began with simply paying attention. He began to live fully as a creature in the created world, and animals, both wild and domesticated, became familiar to him. He noticed worms on the street after a storm, birds in cages who deserved to be free, and fish caught that he would rather set loose than set his teeth into.

He joined a group of pilgrims on a walking journey to Rome, to visit the ancient churches, venerate the saints' relics. He was looking for answers and for enlightenment. While there, he practiced begging alms, one source says, and he exchanged clothes with a poor man.

Back home, he saw the disadvantaged, poor, and rejected outside of Assisi, in the course of his wanderings, and they frightened him. The uncleanliness of their bodies repulsed him. Some of these were lepers, and they especially scared young Francis. What if their condition rubbed off on him? Until one day when Francis turned around. Having rejected a leprous man's appeal in disgust, Francis suddenly turned around and returned to the spot where he stood and embraced him. What enabled him to turn around? Francis had no idea.

Then, one day, this sensitive soul was alone in a mostly abandoned church outside the city walls of Assisi, kneeling in prayer. He was probably there for a long time, quiet. He heard God speak to him. "Rebuild my church," God said, and Francis obeyed that voice by beginning to gather stones. He set to work rebuilding that church. Of course, that was only the beginning, and what started so simply and innocently became a spiritual and social action movement.

Francis's listening, and his hearing and responding, we have to believe those are things that can happen to any one of us.

Life, as we most often live it, is not lively but can feel more like a routine disappointment. What Francis offers stands this on its head. He does this by starting at a different assumption from the typical Christian saint. Sin is not his starting point. Neither is the struggle against evil, which had such a powerful hold on many of his contemporaries. He instead begins with awareness and consciousness: Where are you right now? How do you understand yourself in the world? Because where you are and who you are—before God, among other people, with other creatures—determines what kind of person you will be. What kind of person you will be begins to determine the world in which you live. Francis teaches us to live in reality and to begin to see the One, true Reality.

• • •

For Francis, that One is seen most clearly in the person, life, and teachings of Jesus Christ. When people say that Francis modeled himself after Jesus, it sounds almost trite. Many people have claimed to do such a thing, and Christians seem to roll those words off their tongues with ease, as if "living like Christ" makes obvious sense to everyone, and as if anyone really does it. Preachers in churches every Sunday say this, and people hearing them go home repeating the words, as if they will do it, too. Of course, they don't, really, and they probably never even seriously attempt to grasp what doing so would entail.

In contrast, Francis set out to very literally do what Jesus did and taught, according to the accounts of the Gospels in the New Testament. From selling all that he owned, to sleeping under the stars, to preaching the Gospel to strangers, to being happy to be reviled, he was setting out to imitate the Jesus he knew and to do what he did and taught. It has recently been said: "By his intense poverty, humility, and sufferings, the *Poverello* became a living icon of Christ."[4] That gets at it—at the difference between Francis of Assisi's modeling his life after Jesus and the easy language that makes it seem ordinary. Poverello is a name Francis used for himself. It means, in Italian, "little poor man."

He wasn't the only person, or the first, to begin attempting to follow Christ in ways of personal poverty and simplicity, not even during his era. Christianity was undergoing a change in the century before Francis's birth, which continued during his lifetime, that experts say was equivalent to the change that took place a few centuries later in what is known as the Reformation. The earlier transition—during Francis's life—usually goes unnoticed or unremarked upon. The model of the monk as one who has a specialized religious vocation was breaking down, and new and independent ways of expressing a religious vocation were being founded. Both men and women began to withdraw from the world in ways that were apart from established religious foundations. Many of these new religious went to live in wilderness or desert areas, remembering the origins of monasticism itself, which started in the deserts outside Alexandria, Jerusalem, and Damascus. They remembered, too, Jesus going into the wilderness to be alone with God and to be tempted by the devil.

It became common to see oneself as a faithful disciple of Jesus, even while practicing faith outside of church walls and apart from an established monastic order. This was a radical departure from the status quo. It upset many in authority in the Church. (They became even more upset when some of these independent spiritual practitioners taught heretical ideas. Some called the Cathars became one such group.) But for people like Francis, what was really happening was the birth of what we now know so easily as spirituality.

Soon others began to notice what was happening in and around Francis. I suspect that he was putting off a kind of light or energy that was impossible for more sensitive souls to notice and then resist. But as most of the scholars note: "Francis seemed to be surprised when other men asked to join him." Such foolishness is not usually appreciated. But then, when "they had reached the symbolic number of twelve, Francis and his brothers went to Rome to seek papal confirmation of their form of living."[5] This wasn't withheld by Pope Innocent III, but it also wasn't eagerly granted. There were too many of these new religious orders popping up just then; Innocent would call the Fourth Lateran Council only a few years later, precisely to stem that tide. But Francis and his merry band went away with enough of a blessing to continue with the understanding that Rome didn't mind their lives of poverty and their urging others to likewise live more faithfully to Mother Church.

The next seventeen years would be full of travels, ministries, relationships, and occasional struggles with Church authorities who wanted to curb the earnestness of those first principles. Many of the anecdotes from these years are told in the following pages, and the central characters to appear show up in these stories. They include the highborn St. Clare, the first woman to join the ragtag group in the valley below Assisi, to the disappointment of her uncles, but her sisters and mother would soon join her at the convent they established at San Damiano. And Brother Leo, the simple and loving friend who accompanied Francis on many of his journeys, listening to many of his teachings, and passed them along to the next generation like Aaron did for his brother, Moses. There's St. Anthony of Padua, too, who came to the Franciscans from another religious order after observing some Franciscan friars on the road. Anthony was a great theologian and Francis worried that he not titillate the companions with theological curiosities at the expense of their spiritual passion.

Spirituality was what mattered most to St. Francis, and he was eager to emphasize that a life spiritually tuned was available to every person, wherever they are.

What Francis Accomplished

Francis Bernardone is a figure both in history and in the history of the Spirit, which means that he stands in time but also somewhat outside of his time and place. In this (and only this), St. Francis is like the Buddha and Jesus, and like those earlier figures, he cannot ultimately be understood without looking at the time when he grew up, the environment he was a part of, and how his life was formed by those things and by his desire to make changes.

Many make the mistake of imagining him to be too simple. He's too easily the gnome saint who sits silently in the garden observing the flowers and winged creatures. Francis did simple things, and he was surprised at how widely they were sometimes appreciated. But he was also a complex man with varying motivations who often seemed to contradict himself. For example, he taught his spiritual friends not to get too carried away with their ascetic practices of self-denial, and yet Francis admitted at the end of his life to treating his body like a mule and he was sorry for it. Another example is seen in his style of leadership. The pattern went like this: Francis sets a rule or makes a near decree that something must or mustn't be done by the friars; a friar disobeys by doing or not doing what Francis has made compulsory; Francis punishes or severely corrects the friar; then

Francis is sorry and apologetic for having been so strident and insists that the friar he admonished now punish him. These examples in Francis's life undercut the popular image of him as a hippie saint—an image that became common a generation or two ago. It wasn't the nature of a hippie to deny himself pleasure or to scold those who broke rules.

He was visual. He was dramatic. He was tough. He was shy and uncertain. He was a bundle of contradictions, and I'm convinced it is these contradictions that made him popular then, as well as now. These are some of the ways by which it is difficult to measure his accomplishments. But it is easy to point to two specific ways that he transformed the Church in his day and impacted the world around him.

First, Francis was on the side of the disadvantaged, the poor, the sick, those discarded by society, and those seen as foreign or frightening. In this way, he was exceedingly courageous and taught other Christians not to be afraid of what they don't understand. His efforts at peacemaking were undertaken when Italian cities were rife with public vendettas, private enmities, and thug violence. Making peace between people was never simple. "Peace I leave with you; my peace I give to you," Jesus said in John 14:27, but most people thought those words of their Lord referred to a future heavenly kingdom, rather than something possible here on earth. When peace *was* possible, preachers often asked people to obtain it through penance. From fasts to self-flagellation, the faithful were encouraged to show God their consciousness of sin in the hope that God would bring peace through civil order and protection. Francis's friars were some of the most effective at this and other forms of preaching throughout Europe during the thirteenth century, and Francis himself seemed always most interested in being personally involved. There were courageous saints before Francis, but they were almost always courageous as martyrs: happy to have their lives struck down as witness to faith in Christ. Francis's intrepidity and bravery were different. He placed himself in uncomfortable positions between feuding parties and physical danger between people—in encounters with wild animals and between vowed enemies in wartime situations. We too easily imagine him in statues, with a few fingers gesturing, peace reigning through his holy presence—but that's not how it happened.

The most extravagant example of this courage came in the long journey he undertook to see the Muslim sultan in the Nile Delta during the Fifth Crusade. Nearly every Christian alive viewed a man like the sultan as someone to kill, not someone to love. That is one of the reasons why it was so easy to recruit knights and soldiers to join each new crusade. They'd been going for more than a century. Also in the century before Francis, a powerful Christian monk named Peter the Venerable went to great expense and effort to locate Muslim texts, the Qur'an and its commentaries, and have them translated into Latin for the first time, simply so they could be refuted. Monks and theologians began to carry copies of these translations from place to place, to preach against them. Imagine then, Francis with courage that bordered at times on madness, childlike, remembering the Gospels, naïve, preaching to the sultan in a language the sultan would not even have understood. Francis seems to have believed that if only the Muslim leader could meet and talk with a faithful Christian he might see to changing his ways. That of course didn't happen, but it is no accident that to this day Franciscans take care of most of the holy places in Jerusalem and the Holy Land, safeguarding them with the cooperation and understanding of Jews, Arabs, and Christians.

Second, Francis completely changed how Christians view the natural world and its creatures. What was most often regarded as potentially useful or dangerous, before Francis, was shown to be sanctified in the saint's example and teachings. He showed why and how to be gentle with creatures. He appreciated the wildness of mammals, plants, birds, and fish, knowing that they understood things humans cannot. The twentieth-century anthropologist Claude Lévi-Strauss once said: "It is almost painful for me to know that I will never be able to find out what the matter and structure of the universe is made of. This would have meant being able to talk to a bird. But this is the line that cannot be crossed."[6] Francis attempted to cross that line. Perhaps he succeeded just a little bit. He was also reverent in the face of the stars, the sun, and the moon. He was even careful of stones in a way that suggests all natural things have life and breath. I even wonder if this appreciation of the sacredness of simple things could explain the world we now realize is much larger than humanity. I mean, we now know that the consciousness of human beings is very recent in the history of creation; for billions of years our planet consisted only of single-cell organisms. Did God's involvement only begin with the forming of our first human parents? Of course not. God is without beginning and end. All is sacred and has always been. If only this imagination and vision of Francis, of how human beings interact with the rest of creation, had held sway in the centuries after his death—if only people had followed him on this point—our planet home wouldn't be in the imminent danger today that it finds itself in. Only in the last century have sensitive people caught up to Francis in this.

He also understood the power of symbols—from removing his fancy clothes in front of his father and all of Assisi to lying flat on the ground when he was ill and soon to die. He insisted on doing both of those things. His father's luxurious garments were a symbol of what he wanted to leave completely behind. The soil upon which he lay while dying was a symbol of where his body was soon to go. He life was full of these symbolic gestures.

On another occasion, Francis was asked to preach to the small community of nuns that had formed around St. Clare: he created a circle of ashes and stood in the center of the circle to deliver the Gospel. The gesture itself was the message. More familiar to many of us, the Stations of the Cross and the Nativity crèche each have their origins in the life and teachings of Francis, who realized how powerful it can be to imagine oneself contemporary with Jesus in events such as his Passion and Nativity, in order to love him more completely and identify more fully with his mission.

Often when I consider Francis's life and all its concerns, I find myself making lists of these sorts of words and symbols, each standing for a pivotal moment in his life or one of his teachings. I started my list about twenty years ago. Since then, I have resumed it many times and it has grown. It moves alphabetically and includes items such as these:

Animals—wild and tame, stories of Francis regarding creatures as "brothers" and "sisters." Amazing for his time/era, when animals were understood as either domestic workers or wildly threatening! Underneath this was an understanding of human creatureliness.

Birds—Releasing a dove was his first gesture of conversion. (Sometimes, in the Middle Ages, doves were used by artists to symbolize the first twelve apostles of Christ.) Later, Francis stopped to preach to birds when no one else seemed to want to listen.

Books—Francis disliked monastic book culture. He didn't like to feel the animal skin of a book's cover, and probably most of all, he saw how, in some people, attention to books can displace a passion for God. Compared to the monastic culture that surrounded him in the early thirteenth century, Francis was an iconoclast.

Brown—the color. Not so much brown, but the most drab, ordinary, earthy hue imaginable. This was the color of the clothes he proscribed for himself and all who follow him: the exact opposite of the fancy colored silks he used to market and sell for his father.

Caves—the places of his earliest years of religious life. Solitary places for prayer. It is said that a close friend would often accompany Francis, in the early days, to caves, where the friend would wait outside for hours while the saint prayed in the cool darkness.

Cloisters—places of sure safety in Francis's era (stone walls, negotiated protections, powerful abbots, large stores of food and supplies), rejected by him in favor of a friar's more wandering life of service and uncertainty.

Clowns—one of the descriptors for early Franciscan friars, embraced by Francis. (See *Jugglers*.)

Cross—An icon crucifix was the vehicle by which Francis first heard God speak to him, while he kneeled in the abandoned church of San Damiano in Assisi. (See *Tau*.)

Death—He called her his sister.

Dream—It was said that Pope Innocent III had a dream, after meeting young Francis in Rome, that the great and ancient church of St. John Lateran was falling down and Francis's shoulders were all that were holding it up. Then the pope approved the nascent Franciscan *Rule* and way of life. You can still see the thirteenth-century painter Giotto's rendition of this scene on the wall of the Basilica in Assisi today.

Fathers—Francis viewed his religious life as beginning only when he turned away from his earthly father to embrace what his heavenly Father wanted of him. That's quite a twist on the commandment to honor one's mother and father. Francis never seems to have tried to repair the relationship with his father, after that famous parting from him in front of a crowd in Assisi. Then again, Scripture says: "Can fire be carried in the bosom without burning one's clothes?" (Prov. 6:27). Perhaps sometimes it's impossible to maintain a fire for God without the burning affecting other aspects of life.

Fires—It is said that Francis created fire to impress the sultan with wonders greater than the sultan's magicians could create and that he danced around that fire. The image of Francis dancing around fire captures much of his creative and passionate spirit. At the end of Francis's life, in the "Canticle of the Creatures," he praises Brother Fire.

Fish—Francis was recognized as saintly during his own lifetime. People wanted to meet him, honor him, give things to him. One day, a local fisherman took Francis out in his boat, caught a big fish, and presented it as a gift to the saint. Francis kissed it and let it back into the water. I wonder what the fisherman thought of that.

Jugglers—Francis was dramatic on purpose, calling himself one of God's jongleurs. Jongleurs were entertainers who dressed up in costumes, played funny roles, and made people laugh. They were a form of "low culture," popular in the Middle Ages in France and Italy. To call himself a jongleur was also to link himself with the poor, against the rich, because jongleurs made their reputations poking fun at those in power. Paintings of them from that time are even on the walls of churches.

Knights—what Francis wanted to be, before he first heard God speak to him. What Francis then undermined, quietly, subtly, when he traveled to Egypt to see the sultan during the Crusades.

Mothers—We know almost nothing about Francis's mother, except that she sometimes objected to the harsh treatment he underwent at the hands of her husband. Francis often instructed his friars to be "like mothers" to one another.

Mountains—Francis was gifted a mountain one hundred kilometers north of Assisi in the Tuscan Apennines as a place of refuge and retreat. It was known by the name Laverna, for the goddess of thieves, since it had long been a place where criminals might hide. (Today, the Sanctuary of La Verna sits atop what is now called Mount Penna.)

Nakedness—He stood naked in front of everyone in town when he handed his father his clothes to say he no longer had anything that belonged to him. Look at the famous painting on the wall of the Basilica in Assisi if you don't believe me. The bishop is putting his own coat over Francis's shoulders to cover him up.

Poverty—He wanted to own nothing, not even food, taking seriously the teaching of Jesus not to worry for tomorrow. After Francis's death, the Franciscans were divided on this issue, and there were lengthy arguments as to what Jesus really meant.

Robbers—There was the time when Francis converted robbers by showing them he was not afraid to lose whatever he had, that nothing he had was available to be stolen. You can find that story in a collection of stories about him, *The Little Flowers of Saint Francis.*

Stones—He insisted on being careful with stones, as if they were living creatures with breath. Walk carefully over them, he taught—this in contrast to projects of massive proportions involving stones, just then, as the first Gothic cathedrals were being built in Europe.

Tau—The T-shaped cross image Francis embraced, still representative of Franciscan spirituality. Both image and name come from the last letter in the Hebrew alphabet.

The prophet Ezekiel says that God wanted this symbol used at a time when the sanctuary and holiness of the temple had been violated: "Go through the city, through Jerusalem, and put a mark on the foreheads of those who sigh and groan over all the abominations that are committed in it" (Ez. 9:4).

Tunics—He told his brothers they could own two tunics and they might "lovingly patch" them if they become worn or torn. Pilgrims can see one of his own tunics preserved, still, in the Basilica in Assisi.

Weapons—After his conversion, Francis treated them as unclean things, not to be touched.

Wolves—Brother Wolf is the "brother" whom Francis befriended in the town of Gubbio, when he arranged for the animal to stop harming people and for the townspeople to adequately feed the beast. Some historians have suggested this legendary wolf was actually a human being, the word "wolf" in Italian being *lupo* and there having been a Friar Lupo in the early days who was said to have been a converted criminal.

These are specific images and symbols in Francis's life. There are others less distinct but no less identified with him. There is, for instance, the look of Assisi in the early evening, as the sun begins to set on churches and houses and ancient Roman municipal buildings, reflecting on the pink limestone quarried from Mount Subasio. At night, Subasio can be seen looming over the town just under the light of the moon.

Finally, there is the way in which Francis brought masculine and feminine together in his charism and spiritual vision. This will come through clearly later. And there is his relationship with Clare. You may have seen her in one of the many popular film versions of the life of Francis. Francis and Clare have often been portrayed as passionate young lovers for whom ardor is replaced by a dramatic act of will on Francis's part to love God more completely than any person in his life, even a sweetheart. Those make for good stories, and they've appealed to audiences. They may have a kernel of truth in them, but most likely they're exaggerations of what happened.

There is no question that Francis loved Clare, relied on her, cherished her. And she loved and cherished him. She fled her family home while still a teenager, when her family expected her to marry, and all she wanted was the religious life that Francis had undertaken. Clare was the first woman to join Francis and the others as a "brother." This is why, according to Franciscan history, she and Francis are both described as founders of the Second Order: the women's movement of earliest Franciscans. For a few hours, perhaps a day or two, after her arrival, Clare was one of the guys. There was a woman in the camp. They had to figure out what to do! They soon realized that, particularly at that time, there was no way for men and women to live together in religious life. Clare would soon be joined by other women, including her own sister, in a more cloistered version (according to the demands of that time) of what Francis, Bernard, Leo, and the others were doing.

But Francis always had Clare in his heart and turned to her often for spiritual advice and guidance. Even more, Francis began to embody a way of religious life that was deliberately not masculine-only. His gentleness, as well as his frequent advice to his fellow spiritual brothers, reveals a way of life that embraces ways of following Christ that are influenced by the feminine in him. This is how he advises his brothers, at one point, to "be like mothers" to one another. Such teachings were influenced by his devotion to the Virgin Mary but also from what he was discovering in himself, and in his relationship with Clare.

There is a legend about Francis and Clare that comes from the early days, soon after Clare had set up a cloistered life for herself and other women. The story begins with Clare wanting to spend time with Francis. Like a husband who is too focused on his work, Francis is not making time to share a meal with the woman he loves. This comes to the attention of the men around Francis, who tell their brother he needs to listen to Clare on this matter. He shouldn't be neglecting her for any reason. Francis was probably, again, worried about propriety. What would people think if he was spending too much time with Clare? Finally, a meal between the two was arranged at St. Mary of the Angels, the little chapel Francis had been given below Assisi, around which were spread the early temporary dwellings of the brothers.

While Francis and Clare sat picnicking and talking, they must have been reminiscing and laughing and even crying with happiness. The energy around them was electric, as it always had been, as it always would be. But, as the story goes, the people of Assisi—up in the town—saw something else when they looked down in the valley, in the direction of St. Mary of the Angels. It was said that flames of fire were seen. Assisians ran with containers of water to help put out the flames. But when they arrived, of course, all they saw was the love and friendship of Francis and Clare together. Francis was able to bring this energy into himself and to love others in ways that were more than what was normally seen in a man.

These are aspects of Francis's legacy that have been undervalued, even suppressed, in official treatments of the saint. The official biography by St. Bonaventure, for instance, does not even mention the "Canticle of the Creatures." Bonaventure wrote his official biography forty years after Francis's death. The saint's earthiness, too, is hidden from view. In many of the official treatments, only the penitent sinner who becomes a faithful son of the Church, and the mystic, is clearly viewed.

A Protestant writer named Paul Sabatier began to rediscover the real, radical, gentle Francis with a biography in the 1890s that then became a bestseller around the world. It is a book that I reedited and presented anew nearly twenty years ago as *The Road to Assisi*. In Italy, Chiara Mercuri has done similarly just recently, titling her biography, *Francis of Assisi: The Hidden Story*. It is being translated into English now. It is essential to move beyond what Bonaventure offers in the "official" treatment, which is a mystical Francis who is impossible to emulate. Instead, when we look more closely, we can see the real man and saint who inspires people still to discover and experience the living God in the world around them.

Francis's Teachings

St. Francis of Assisi, like Jesus before him, possessed a simple message. They emphasized transformed living and everyday spiritual practice over forms of doctrine. The French philosopher Pascal once wrote about Jesus: "He said great things so simply that he seems not to have thought about them, and yet so clearly that it is obvious what he thought about them. Such clarity together with such simplicity is wonderful" (*Pensées,* 309). The same could be said of Francis.

Francis was not remembered for his preaching the way Jesus was. Relatively little of what Francis said in sermons seems to have been written down or remembered, and that says something about what the sermons were probably like. I suspect it also says something about the content and style of the sermons: they were not moments that impressed an audience or expanded people's knowledge in matters of doctrine.

They were, more simply, reminders (visual and oral, given Francis's ways of communicating) of what people had once heard the Gospel to be about.

When Francis found himself starting a new religious and spiritual movement, much to his surprise, he surely had no idea that what was leading to the incredible appeal of his message was its very simplicity. The sort of preaching and teaching that Francis was doing was unusual for his time. Showing and talking the Gospel was refreshing. This helps to explain why we have relatively little of Francis's writings. Francis was similar to other great spiritual teachers in history, in this regard—figures such as Socrates, the Greek philosopher; the Baal Shem Tov, initiator of Jewish Hasidism; and Lakota medicine man and Catholic catechist Nicholas Black Elk, who left no writings behind at all. In the stories of Francis, we most often see him handling situations in ways that didn't result in much talk. You can sense him trying to avoid formal teaching when possible. He looked to the heart of things, and his actions spoke louder than his words.

So we have relatively little by way of writings from Francis's hand, but we have some—and what we have is precious. He wrote letters, admonitions, well wishes, songs, and even a spiritual testament at the end of his life. Sometimes he had another act as a scribe while he dictated, because he was ill or perhaps because he wasn't adept at reading and writing. He was conscious of needing to get certain things down on paper, for the sake of others. We even have a couple instances of Francis's actual handwriting. But few people, then, were writing things down. There were theologians who wrote books for their students, and there were scribes and students and royal assistants who wrote down what popes or bishops or royalty had to say. But almost no one else was writing. Francis was mostly a poet, and poets sang rather than wrote. Much of what you'll read here from St. Francis probably began as song.

He was no bookish saint. There are plenty of those. We probably don't need more. In the iconography of St. Francis, you'll never see him holding a pen or a book. St. Anne, the mother of the Virgin Mary, holds a book because of the legends of her instructing her daughter in the Scriptures. St. John, the Gospel writer, holds a book in his hands because he wrote one or two. It's difficult to find a holy image or saint card of St. Augustine, author of *The City of God* and *Confessions,* two of the most important books in the history of Christianity, without pen or book in hand. And there are lots of others. But not Francis—look at holy images of him and you'll see him with a wolf, with fish, with birds, holding a skull, or with stigmata wounds. It would have been just like Francis to say to someone who reads one of the following documents, *Now that you've read what I've written, put the paper away. Go live!* He was more like the holy men and women of ancient cultures who knew what they knew by heart and taught it by example than the theologians and spiritual authors of his own Catholic tradition.

But there were still people around who, after a while, began to realize they might want to write down what Francis was saying. Certainly no one was doing that in the early years. Why would anyone walk beside the young man the whole town thought crazy, jotting things down? No one would! But thank God, eventually, they did begin to write down some of it. And once his way of spiritual practice was established, Francis needed and wanted certain things to be recorded, to be kept, remembered. This is why he wrote letters to people, bits of formal advice to his spiritual brothers, even a rule of life, which was common among all monastic and religious orders, and he came to realize that he was creating a new one.

Supplementing these are the oral teachings that were written down after Francis's death. There are many such fragments that have been collected over the centuries, and several of these appear later in this book as well.

Some of what's been attributed to Francis is not always accurate. For example, one of the most common quotations of St. Francis you'll find is one he never actually said—or at least, he didn't say it as it is quoted: "Preach the Gospel at all times, only occasionally, use words." What he did in fact say was "God has called us with so much mercy, not only for our souls, but for others'. So we should be out in the world encouraging people, always more by deeds than by words. Show them how you do penance for your sins and how you live the commandments." He said this early in his conversion and very early in his public ministry. He was doing Gospel things, receiving confused looks from the people of Assisi who'd watched him transform from a frivolous child to a wisdom seeker and God wrestler before their eyes. This is to illustrate how he lived his teachings more than he spoke or wrote them. And this is why a collection of Francis's writings that includes only what we know to have come directly from him is as thin as a book of poems.

He distrusted written words, or at least written words that were not Scripture, because Scripture words he revered like holy objects, almost superstitiously. When he would encounter a piece of paper or parchment with Latin writing—the language of Scripture in those days, which Francis couldn't read—he would reverently pick it up and put it in a safe place. He tells us this himself in his "Testament" (see later in this book): "If I ever find our Lord's holy names, or any piece of writing sitting around, I gather them and take them to a more holy place." Words were not in common currency. There were no spiritual books other than those locked away in monastery scriptoriums, or the commissioned personal breviaries (prayer books) of wealthy people. This is why some of Francis's writings appear overly simple. See "Our Simple Rule of Life," for instance.

He showed little interest in numbers, either. Living when numbers were central to conceptualizing knowledge, Francis didn't seem to notice. Peter Lombard's *Four Books of Sentences* (*Libri Quattuor Sententiarum*) was the essential reading for theological students. There were also four humors to explain human emotion (blood, yellow bile, black bile, and phlegm), four evangelists, and from ancient philosophy to medieval alchemy there were four elements. Then there was the number seven: days in the story of Creation, years of feast and then famine, archangels, sorrows of the Virgin, deadly sins, gifts of the Holy Spirit, metals, liberal arts. Not to mention three: floors of Noah's ark, mysterious visitors to Abraham, days Jonah remained in the whale's belly, magi visiting the Christ child, persons of the Godhead. And so on. Francis's use of numbers was always practical and according to earlier religious traditions. Every Franciscan should make a confession of sins at least three times a year, for instance, and a typical punishment for a simple offense is to say three Our Fathers. Francis is clear to say that God is to be understood in three persons. "All three have come down among us," he says in his "Singing the Virgin Mary's Praises" (see later in this book).

Most of Francis's teaching is about acquiring new ways of looking at life that lead to changes in how one lives. We come to these teachings with typical assumptions (twenty-first-century assumptions are probably little different from thirteenth-century ones), and one by one Francis dismantles them. What we thought was true simply is not, and the Gospel of Jesus offers the corrective.

For example, is the purpose of life simply survival? It isn't, says Francis, and of course on this and every point Francis is repeating or reframing the Gospel. Life is not for survival; it is for joy. There is a way of living that is freer, fresher, and more satisfying than focusing on simply how to get through the day. Flip survival on its head: embrace your death, instead. By dying to the illusions that the world teaches, we even begin to see how to weather stormy times and disappointments. They don't matter so much after all.

Is the way to happiness security? Again, no, says Francis. And again, the opposite is true. Christianity can fill the hills and valleys with thick-walled monasteries, but Francis preferred to sleep in a cave or lean-to. He created the walkabout friar. Kings, princes, even popes, parents, and abbots, will disappoint you, he knew, but God will not. The way to God, for Francis, was through the Church and the sacraments, but Francis emphasized that there was so much more besides.

Is church the place to find God? God is there without a doubt, Francis says, but God is discovered everywhere, Francis adds, and there have always been Catholics and other Christians who have found that uncomfortable. Francis is the world's most popular saint, however, and saints have always been people of the people. So the People of God say Francis was correct. Look for God in more places than church.

It is impossible to overemphasize how radical this was. In the face of a discarded leper. In the dance of a child. In wolves and worms and weasels. Among God's many discarded creatures, who, despite being discarded by the world, experience their Creator whenever they praise him. It is easier to understand Francis's teaching on this point today than it was when he taught it eight hundred years ago. For instance, today there are scientists who talk of the world as "kincentric" (and folklorists say this idea goes back to the earliest human beings), which means that "animals, even plants, whatever lives, moves, or breathes, are near relatives."[1]

Speaking to mammals and birds, trees and fish, like equals was radical in Francis's day. Such a view was opposed by the Catholic Church even 350 years later when they put Montaigne's *Essays* on the index of forbidden books simply because the philosopher argued animals were rational creatures.

But there were limits to this God-in-the-world mysticism. Interpreters of St. Francis sometimes make too much of it and he becomes separated from his religious tradition. The mystical saint is impossible to emulate, when Francis the Teacher shows a clear path.

At the end of his life, Francis seemed less sure of himself, not more. Regardless of his mystical stigmata experience, when it is said a vision of the risen Christ pierced Francis with wounds similar to those of Christ, Francis kept asking questions. He wanted to emphasize where he is most certain of God's presence in the world, and he does that in his final piece of writing, "The Testament" (see later in this book). There he writes:

> I am only able to see the Son of God clearly, in this corporeal world, in his holy Body and Blood, which only priests may administer. This is the one holy mystery to be honored above all others.

There are many riches in Francis's writings, and they speak as clearly today as they did when he wrote them.

A PRAYER FOR GOD'S PRESENCE

DATE: 1206

GENRE: PRAYER

His earliest recorded prayer or spiritual writing, these words were first prayed by Francis, according to biographers, while he kneeled alone in front of an icon of Christ that still hangs in Assisi today. Francis spoke these words to God while kneeling in an abandoned church, passionately wanting to know from God what to do with his life.

Highest of all,
Most beautiful One,
Please enlighten my heart, even in the shadows,
Where I try to hide.

Please show me the right and true way
To follow you,
With confidence and hope,
With love and a feeling of understanding of
You and your presence in my life?

Only then, will I be able to do
Your holy will and follow
Your true commandments.
Amen.

When Francis heard God respond, "Go and rebuild my church," one can't overstate how far the idea of starting a religious order was, at that moment, from his thoughts.

OUR SIMPLE RULE OF LIFE

DATE: 1209

GENRE: MONASTIC RULE, CARRIED IN THE POCKETS OR MEMORIES OF THE FIRST FRANCISCANS

No one has ever found a copy of this document, but we know that when Francis and the first friends who joined him in vows of poverty, chastity, and obedience walked to Rome to present themselves to Pope Innocent III, they had constructed a few essential rules for their way of life, and they carried this with them. As Francis tells us later in his "Testament" (see later in this book), "I wrote it all down very simply, using few words, to show the Pope, who confirmed it for me." He knew, then, the source of their charisma or spirit. These rules also might have been, very simply, memorized. Medieval people memorized much more easily than we do today. You can almost see Francis saying—or "performing"—these principles of life for the pope.

In any case, that first Franciscan "Rule" has never been found in document form. After returning from Rome, Francis and those around him (mostly those around him) redacted, edited, and built upon these simple outlines to create what came to be known as "The Rule of Life of 1223" (see later); it guides the way of life for Franciscans still today.

When reading this one, imagine the simple friar from the anecdote in the introduction to this book who was mocked by kids in the piazza until someone finally sat beside him and said, "What are you doing here? Who are you?" What he pulled from his cowl pocket might have looked like this:

Our Rule of Life is very simple: poverty, chastity, obedience. Follow the teachings—and the very footsteps!—of Jesus Christ our Lord.

Jesus is the one who said these things:

"If you wish to be perfect, go, sell your possessions, and give the money to the poor, and you will have treasure in heaven; then come, follow me." Gospel of St. Matthew 19:21

"If any want to become my followers, let them deny themselves and take up their cross daily and follow me." Gospel of St. Luke 9:23

"Whoever comes to me and does not hate father and mother, wife and children, brothers and sisters, yes, and even life itself, cannot be my disciple." Gospel of St. Luke 14:26

"And everyone who has left houses or brothers or sisters or father or mother or children or fields, for my name's sake, will receive a hundredfold, and will inherit eternal life." Gospel of St. Matthew 19:29

TO THOSE WHO WANT TO JOIN OUR WAY OF LIFE

DATE: UNDATED; LIKELY 1209–10

GENRE: EXHORTATION OR ENCOURAGEMENT

The Franciscans are the most numerous religious order in the world, and that began eight hundred years ago. People were drawn to Francis in startlingly large numbers, from the earliest days. They must have recognized the authenticity of his conversion—and they were drawn to the way of life he was beginning to follow. This text, presented here in shorter version than it is often found, finds Francis expanding beyond what was stated in "Our Simple Rule of Life," summarizing more of what one must do to be a faithful follower of Jesus Christ in the Franciscan way (and, he suggests, to be a happy human being):

Happy and blessed are the men and women who love the Lord with all their heart, soul, mind, and strength, and who love their neighbors as themselves.

They are happy and blessed who put away sinful ways, who receive the Body and Blood of Christ in the mass, and begin to show the fruits that come through penance.

The Spirit of God has come to rest on these people, and is making a home among them for eternity. These are God's children. They have become as the husbands, wives, brothers, sisters, and mothers of our Lord Jesus.

We are the husbands and wives of Jesus when the Holy Spirit has joined us to him.

We are brothers and sisters to Jesus when we do the will of God in heaven.

We are mothers of Jesus if we carry him in our hearts and lives by living in holy ways, shining in this world for and on behalf of others.

Those who do not do these things, and do not become God's own, I am sorry to say, are being held like prisoners, blind and deceived, by the devil. They may think that they possess the vanities of this world, but they do not, and what they believe is theirs, will only one day be taken from them. I pray that they will soon, quickly, find the true spirit and life that is in Jesus.

SINGING MOTHER MARY'S PRAISES

DATE: UNDATED

GENRE: SONG OR POEM

While he was finding his way, Francis developed a devotion to the Virgin Mary that was typical of the saints of his day, but also deeply personal and passionate. Francis never did anything halfheartedly.

When we read these words today, flat on the page, we need to imagine how Francis composed them. Not on paper. He most likely *imagined these words while standing before icons of Mary in churches, stopping to pray the daily Angelus (*Angelus Domini nuntiavit Mariæ, *"The angel of the Lord declared unto Mary"), while walking in the fields of Assisi seeing the flowers and plants that are named for her (e.g., lily of the valley), and while singing. These words were sung by Francis, not just spoken or read:*

Adore the Holy Woman!
Love our most blessed queen, Mary.
She was, and is, the only Mother of God.

Our Lady is set apart forever.
She was chosen by God the Father.
She was made holy by God the Son.
She was inspired by the Holy Ghost.

These holy Three have come down among us,
And remain with us still
Our grace and source of every goodness.

So give honor to God's quiet palace.
Offer praise to God's beautiful tabernacle.
We thank you, robe of God, servant of God,
Mother of our one and only God.

RULES FOR LIVING ALONE

DATE: 1217

GENRE: EXHORTATION OR ENCOURAGEMENT

This exceedingly simple piece of writing demonstrates a tension that Francis experienced in his own life: feeling torn between the quiet life of a hermit, which affords so much opportunity for contemplation and prayer, and the communal life to which he felt most called. Early in Francis's conversion, while he was spending long hours praying by himself in a cave above the town of Assisi, he began to feel this tension. He asked two of his closest companions—Brother Sylvester and Sister Clare—to pray for him on this point. He asked them for advice, too. They came back to him and confirmed God's will that Francis was supposed to spend most of his time with and for others.

So here we have a series of rules for early companions who have a similar desire. It turned out that there were several who felt this same tension in their lives. When the religious impulse takes hold, this is common. One wants more and more of the sweetness that one feels alone with God. At the same time, the early Franciscans were about action.

Among us there are some who desire to be and live alone. They may do this for periods of time, living in religious hermitages, but they should not be entirely alone. They should live in numbers of three or four.

Each brother may have his own room to pray in solitude, and to sleep. But he must not always be alone.

In each situation, two of the four brothers should be as "mother" to the other two. The other two, then, should be as "sons." The two who are being as mothers for their sons should follow the life of Martha, from holy scripture, and the sons who relate to their mothers, should follow the life of Mary.

The friars should recite Compline together daily, beginning immediately after sunset, and then each should be silent.

Rising for Matins, each one could say the hours in the morning, seeking "first the kingdom of God and his righteousness." Gospel of St. Matthew 6:33. He could then also recite Prime at the appointed hour. And then he could end his silence after Terce, when those who are sons may once again go to counsel with their mothers.

When necessary, everyone should ask in humility for their daily bread, just as the poor must do. We should always desire nothing for ourselves but the love of God.

Brothers who live alone like this must never allow someone to enter or eat within their private room. And those brothers who are as mothers to their children should always be seeking to protect their sons from all harm. This includes unnecessary talking—don't do it. And the brothers who are as sons to their mothers should refrain from talking with anyone else but mother, excepting the minister or custodian of the order itself, whom they may visit if they ever need to.

Finally, those who are like a spiritual son should, from time to time, take on the role of spiritual mother. Brothers living in these situations of holy quiet can learn to take turns in these roles by agreement among themselves.

Always try to follow these instructions for holy living apart from the larger communities, as best you can.

LETTER TO ONE WHO RULES OVER OTHERS

DATE: 1220

GENRE: LETTER

As we've seen, Francis was always most concerned with actions and practice over words and doctrine. Later you will see that he wrote in the last section of "The Rule of Life (1223)" that not every companion is designed for preaching and that preaching shouldn't become a friar's full-time work. (In religious orders, full-time preaching often led to problems, including abuses of authority.) Francis wanted every companion of his to be meek; he writes in "The Rule of Life:" "Every brother . . . needs to preach by his deeds."

Francis used preaching to say what other Christian leaders seemed to find it difficult to say to the powerful. This letter is such an occasion, and it probably mirrors what was being said by Francis in sermons at the time. He begins by reminding the recipient—and anyone else who is listening—that he is writing as a small and humble man. (This reminds me a bit of the sandal-footed, robe-wearing Gandhi on the streets of London going to meet the King of England . . . just before the British pulled out of India.)

Just a small, humble servant of God, I am insignificant brother Francis, writing to you today. I wish you every peace. I want you to be well, all of you who are mayors, business leaders, magistrates, and governors in this world of ours, and I wish the same for all who will follow you with various responsibilities.

But, please, take the time to pause and reflect. Consider how the day will soon come when your death approaches. Why is this important? Because our Lord Jesus must not be forgotten, and the commandments of God must not be ignored. I beg you not to forget, and not to ignore this—for those who do so have left the service of God and lost consciousness, and this will carry them into oblivion, cursed and far away from God in the world to come. When death comes, and it will, all that the proud and powerful believe they possess will be stripped from them. They may have been proud and powerful in this world, but in the next they will endure the pains of hell.

So, please, good lords, reflect carefully on your lives and your actions. Don't neglect to receive the Body and Blood of our Lord Jesus. Fervently remember him in all you do.

And help those whom you govern and order that they may be allowed to serve our Lord with praise and thanksgiving. They rely on you. You have responsibilities toward them. If you don't allow them to honor the Lord, you will hear of this from Jesus Christ himself on the day of judgment.

May those who read these words, keep them close at hand, and observe them all their days. They will be blessed by God.

WHAT TO DO TO FOLLOW JESUS

DATE: UNCERTAIN; LIKELY 1220–22

GENRE: EXHORTATION OR ENCOURAGEMENT

Sometimes this piece of writing is titled "Letter to the Faithful." It is, in many respects, an elaborated version of "To Those Who Want to Join Our Way of Life." Like that earlier one, this is presented here in slightly abbreviated form.

This was written about one decade later than "To Those Who Want to Join Our Way of Life," once Franciscanism was in full flower. On a basic level, like the earlier writing, this was produced in response to people asking Francis what to do to follow Jesus. One would think it might have become clear by that point, but apparently not! The answers must have seemed to Francis too obvious to put into words, at first, but then he did so. The contents of this exhortation would have been circulated, copied, and shared from person to person.

The way of St. Francis has become more personal to Francis himself, and his transmission of it is more self-conscious here than it was before.

This is Brother Francis, your servant, sending my peace and love and regard for all of you who sincerely love the Lord, whether you are clergy or laity, men or women, and wherever you live throughout the world. I am your servant. It has been entrusted to me to share the beautiful words of God with all of you.

I cannot visit each of you in person. My body is weaker than it once was. For this reason alone, this piece of writing will have to suffice. May it contain the words of the Holy Spirit, the giver of all spirit and life!

Our Father in heaven chose a holy, glorious woman, the Virgin Mary, to bring forth in human frailty our Savior. Such glorious poverty the world has never seen, and such poverty we must emulate.

Then, in his Passion, that same Lord who was born in poverty, blessed and broke his body for us. He who was born for us, gave himself for us, leaving an example for us then to follow in his very footprints.

We must respond to this gift with the holiness of our lives. This is also the answer to the meaning of life itself. Taste the sweetness of the Lord! Those who do not, I am very sorry to say, will find themselves one day in darkness.

But happy and blessed are the ones who love God with all their heart and mind, and who love their neighbor as themselves. Keep loving him with as pure a heart and mind as you can muster, and pray always, "Our Father, Who art in heaven . . ."

Confess your sins to a priest. Receive the Body and Blood in the mass. Prepare to enter the kingdom of God.

Do penance so as to show the fruits that come of it in your lives—most of all, the love you show to others. Be charitable. Show humility. Give alms to those in need. Fast, and keep away from the vices and sins of too much food and drink.

Visit churches and care for them. Show respect to the clergy, not just because they are clergy, but because they are so close to the Body and Blood of Jesus. Remember always that no one can be saved without that Body and Blood.

Love your enemies, don't curse them. Do good things for those who want to harm you.

Consider your death always. What would you do today if you knew you might die tomorrow? Our bodies are bound for worms.

Do not desire fame, but seek humility. The Spirit of God rests on ordinary people. They are the husbands and wives, brothers and sisters, of Jesus.

All the men and women who do not do these things, I fear for them. They are serving the world and its vanities. They are losing their souls, and what they believe is theirs will soon be taken from them.

I am your brother Francis, your servant, and I kiss your feet, begging you to listen to these words from God. Receive and practice them. May you know the Father, Son, and Holy Spirit, and may you persevere to the very end.

Amen.

TEACHING ON GRATITUDE

DATE: UNDATED

GENRE: ORAL TEACHING

There are many oral teachings of Francis that were written down by the friars after his death. These are memories of what Francis used to often say, elaborating on their Rule, *or teachings offered during general conferences when all the friars were gathered in one place, or simply while Francis was walking along on the road with one of his brothers.*

This is one of those oral teachings that recurs over and over again:

Wherever we are, and wherever we find ourselves, let us consider each other's needs and concerns, physically and spiritually, with diligence and care.

Let's honor each other always without complaining, or whispering about one another.

And let's be especially careful not to walk around looking sad or depressed. Wherever we are, whatever our place and situation, we should be rejoicing and grateful to the Lord for all the good.

TEACHING ABOUT SICKNESS

DATE: UNDATED

GENRE: ORAL TEACHING

Here is another teaching of Francis that was remembered by his spiritual brothers and written down after his death. One must remember that Francis himself acknowledged, at the end of his life, that he may not have always struck the correct balance between care for himself and concern for what is eternal:

Please, brothers, when you are ill, keep thanking God for the good. Praise him and tell him you desire whatever is his holy will for your life. God uses mysterious ways to teach us life's verities, and we may not understand. But praise him!

Don't be angry, brothers, when you are sick—don't be angry with God, and don't be angry with one another. Your wellness is in God's hands, and if you are never well again, please remember that the flesh can be the enemy of the soul. You are bound for eternal life.

TEACHINGS ON OWNING AND POSSESSING THINGS

DATE: UNDATED

GENRE: ORAL TEACHING

Wherever you find yourself, wherever you are laying your head, do not defend it against anyone. Whoever may come, whether a friend or an enemy, even one who simply likes to steal, do not contend with him. It is not yours.

The only things you own in this world are your vices and your sins.

If this feels arduous for you, always remember how you have given yourself completely to God's service. For the sake of our Lord Jesus, you are supposed to endure trials and difficulties, perhaps even death. Why does this worry you, when our Lord himself says, "For those who want to save their life will lose it, and those who lose their life for my sake will save it"? Gospel of St. Luke 9:24

TEACHING ON GUARDING YOUR HEART

DATE: UNDATED

GENRE: ORAL TEACHING

Beware, brothers: The Evil One is wily and skillful, and he does not want anyone to turn toward God. He prowls like a lion seeing prey. He wants to get you in his claws. He wants your resolve and your heart, and he will do what it takes to capture them. Don't listen to him! He will lie and deceive you. He will preoccupy you with worldly concerns. He will tell you that an unclean heart is just fine. It is not. Guard your heart, and keep your mind upon our Lord.

I beg you, put away everything that distracts you from our Lord. Make a home for him inside of you. "Be alert at all times, praying that you may have the strength to escape all these things that will take place, and to stand before the Son of Man." Gospel of St. Luke 21:36

Adore him with purity in your heart and intentions. "And call no one your father on earth, for you have one Father—the one in heaven." Gospel of St. Matthew 23:9

TEACHING ON HOW TO BEHAVE TOWARD UNBELIEVERS

DATE: UNDATED

GENRE: ORAL TEACHING

He speaks of this, too, in "The Rule of Life (1223)," below. Such teaching shows Francis as way ahead of his time when it came to interfaith conversation. Most Christians have not yet learned this lesson from him. . . .

There are two acceptable ways you might behave among those who do not believe the Gospel.

First, keep silent. Don't argue. Look upon others as God's very own, regardless of what they may or may not profess.

Second, and only if you sense that the Holy Spirit is clearly guiding you to do so, you may announce God's word to them, asking them to consider God the Father, God the Son, and God the Holy Spirit. There they may meet the One who creates, and redeems, and inspires all creatures. If they believe, baptize them and they will become Christians.

LETTER TO A MINISTER

DATE: 1221

GENRE: LETTER

We have no idea the identity of the recipient of this letter, but it was clearly someone Francis knew—probably a guardian, or spiritual leader, of other Franciscans in one of the new provinces in Europe. We also don't have the letter Francis was responding to, but it seems it may have been a request for a transfer or a request to leave and seek out a quieter form of spiritual life.

My dear brother, minister, may God bless and keep you. I write this today, as best I can, with concerns for your soul.

Whatever it is that seems to be keeping you from loving God with all your heart, and whoever seems to have become an obstacle to you in that love of God, whether it is one of our friars or anyone else, you should consider this a gift of God's grace. You may not have wanted this obstacle, but God does. This time of your trouble, you should understand to be both a grace and an opportunity for you to show your obedience to him.

You should love anyone who harms or bothers you. You shouldn't be wishing them harm, or even for them to go away. Only God's will be done. In fact, you shouldn't even wish for them to be better Christians, as if that is your judgment to make. It is not.

This is a time for you to go deeply into your private room and pray. If you have done that, then you would see, with God's help, that there is no one in the world who has sinned, or could sin, in such a way as to not merit your forgiveness. And even if he hasn't asked for your forgiveness, you should be asking him if he would like to have it from you. Then, if he continues to hurt or harm you, you are to love him even more. Doing this will draw you even closer to our Lord.

Always be merciful, always. And please share with other ministers, whenever you can, that this is how you are living toward those who hurt or harm you.

I hope that you will keep this letter with you until we are all together at Pentecost, and then you can share it with your brother ministers. With the help of God, we can care for each other in these ways.

THE RULE OF LIFE

DATE: 1223

GENRE: MONASTIC RULE, PRESERVED IN WRITING

As noted in the introduction to "Our Simple Rule of Life," earlier in this book, this later one is the Franciscan Rule that was fully redacted and refined by Francis and those around him in leadership. (Francis gave up leadership of his order in 1220, in part because it was moving away from his original ideals regarding poverty. At this time, he was no longer the leader of the Franciscans.)

Many of the chapters of this version, which is much longer and more detailed, since it needed to address issues facing a large and growing religious order, resemble those found in other monastic rules, on subjects that weren't part of the original spirit of Francis.

CHAPTER 1

In the name of our Lord, this should be the beginning of the way of life of everyone who desires to be a little brother, a Friar Minor.

Our rule and way of life for observing the holy Gospel of Jesus Christ is found in obedience, poverty, and chastity. Brother Francis vows absolute obedience and reverence to Pope Honorius, and to each of his successors who are canonically elected, and to the Roman Catholic Church. Let every friar, then, obey Brother Francis and each of his successors in our way of life.

CHAPTER 2

If someone desires to adopt our way of life and join us, this is what they do.

First of all, send them to see the provincial minister, for it is the minister's responsibility in every province to receive new friars. It is the minister's job to examine a candidate carefully in matters of faith and sacrament. If the candidate is found to believe all things, to profess them, and to express the desire and wish to practice them to the end of days, and if he is unmarried (or his wife has already entered a convent), then he should be addressed with the words of the holy Gospel: "Jesus said to him, 'If you wish to be perfect, go, sell your possessions, and give the money to the poor, and you will have treasure in heaven; then come, follow me.'" Gospel of St. Matthew 19:21. If the candidate cannot do this when it is asked of him, his good will to do so may perhaps suffice.

Neither ministers nor brothers should become too involved in the affairs of candidates and newcomers to our way of life regarding these matters. Each man must and will dispose of his property and goods as our Lord inspires him to do. If counseling becomes necessary, to find the most appropriate ways and manner for accomplishing it, the minister should send a God-fearing person to help guide the candidate in godly ways of distributing his goods to the poor.

Only when this is accomplished, should the clothes of our life be given to the candidate for a year of formation: two tunics without hoods, a cord, pants, and one small cape that attaches to the cord. The minister, however, is permitted to do otherwise if it is in his wisdom, before God, to do so. When the year of formation is concluded, the man should be received into obedience, making a promise to observe this Rule and our way of life. He is then a friar, and one of us, forever, for as the Holy Gospel says, "No one who puts a hand to the plow and looks back is fit for the kingdom of God." Gospel of St. Luke 9:62

Once he has promised obedience, he may have one tunic with a hood, and another, if necessary, without. And only those who out of necessity must wear shoes, may have them. All the friars should always wear coarse garments, and they may lovingly mend them, as necessary, with other pieces of cloth, for God's glory. Still, Brother Francis reminds all never to look down upon those who they see dressed in finer clothes, or taking good food and drink; let every friar only judge himself.

CHAPTER 3

How to pray the Divine Office, how to fast, and how to travel through the world.

Any friar who is also a priest or deacon should say the Divine Office according to the use set by the Roman Catholic Church, with the exception of the Psalter. To do this effectively, they may possess prayer books. Those friars who are laymen should be saying each day twenty-four Our Fathers for matins; five for lauds; seven for each of the hours of prime, terce, sext, and none; twelve for vespers, and seven for compline. They should also be praying for the dead.

Every friar should fast from the Feast of All Saints until the Feast of the Nativity. Other fasts are voluntary, and may God bless those who fast during the Lent that begins at Epiphany and lasts the forty days that our Lord fasted. Let everyone fast, however, during the other Lent, from Ash Wednesday for forty days until our Lord's Resurrection. There is also fasting on Fridays. And during times of special needs, ministers may release brothers from fasting.

Brother Francis counsels and advises his brothers in Jesus Christ, that when they are out in the world they should not argue or judge others. They should be meek and peaceful, gentle and humble. They should speak courteously. They also should not ride a horse unless they must, by necessity, or because of infirmity or illness. And when they enter a house, they should say, "Peace be in this house." And, according to the Gospel of our Lord, they should eat whatever food is put before them.

CHAPTER 4

On avoiding money.

This point is irrefutable by all. No brother is ever permitted to receive coins or money, either themselves or for someone else. Only the ministers and custodians may accept, from friends in the Spirit, provisions and other goods that are needed to care for the sick and clothe the friars according to the seasons of the year. They should do so as they deem necessary—with one exception: they, too, may never ever receive coins or money.

CHAPTER 5

On the subject of work.

If a brother has been given the grace by God to do work, he should do it faithfully and with devotion. Avoid idleness—it is the soul's enemy—and as you work, do not forget the Spirit that inspires us still and always to pray. As payment for work, brothers may receive what is needed for their bodily needs, and those of their fellow brothers, but again, never coin or money. Work humbly. Remember your poverty. Be a servant of God.

CHAPTER 6

Keep no possessions.

Nothing, no stuff, not a house, no place of residence, nothing at all, is to be considered your own. You are pilgrims and strangers in the world. You serve the Lord with humility, in poverty. Ask for alms with confidence that the Lord will always provide for your needs, and that he knows your needs are no more than those of himself when he was one of the poorest of the poor in this world. This is your portion, and it will lead you to heaven.

Wherever you are, and go, meet each other as if you are members of one family. Share your needs with one another. Just as a mother loves a son in the flesh, you should love each other in the spirit. And if one of you becomes ill, the others should care for him as they would also want to be cared for.

CHAPTER 7

Necessary penance for those who sin.

If a brother is influenced by the enemy and commits a mortal sin, he should be sent to his minister, who should then talk with him right away. A minister, whose heart should be full of mercy, must impose a penance on that brother. Without anger or undue passion, the minister who imposes penance should remember always, charity.

CHAPTER 8

Electing a general minister of this order.

There should always be a general minister of this order who is the servant of all the brothers, and to whom all the brothers are bound by obedience. When that general minister dies, let another be elected in his place when the provincial ministers and custodians meet at the Chapter of Pentecost. And, in any case, there should be a general chapter meeting at least once every three years.

If it ever appears that the general minister is unfit to serve the welfare of all the brothers, the provincial ministers and custodians should meet to replace him, for God's sake.

And each provincial minister, after the Chapter of Pentecost, may want to convene a chapter of the brothers in their province to meet that same year.

CHAPTER 9

On preaching.

Friars should never preach where they are not wanted. Listen to the bishops of each diocese and do as they say. Also, every brother should preach as guided by his minister. Finally, when you preach, I, Brother Francis, ask you to please use language that is holy and thoughtful, used for the benefit of edifying your listeners, revealing to them the punishment for vice, and the glory that comes with virtue, and do not preach too long, because our Lord himself, when he was on earth, kept his words brief and to the point.

CHAPTER 10

Warnings for the brothers.

Humbly and with charity, correct one another. Guide one another in what is good for the soul and according to our holy Rule. Each brother, remember that you are subject to your fellow brothers. We have all renounced our rights to govern our own will. So obey each other in all the ways you have promised to obey our Lord and according to our Rule.

If a brother ever feels that he cannot observe the Rule, he should go see his minister. Ministers should, in such cases, practice extreme charity, kindness, and familiarity with the questioning brother. Ministers: remember that you are servants of the brothers, even then.

Every brother, beware of pride and vanity, envy and greed, and caring too much for the things of this world. Do not complain and become distracted. Elevate prayer in your lives more than learning. The illiterate, for instance, shouldn't rush off to school, and never at the expense of their more holy desires to be present to the Holy Spirit and pursuant of God's holy activity. Pray continually. Have pure hearts. Be humble and patient. Endure persecution whenever necessary. Love those who hurt you, and remember our Lord's words: "I say to you, Love your enemies and pray for those who persecute you. Blessed are those who are persecuted for righteousness' sake, for theirs is the kingdom of heaven. You will be hated by all because of my name. But the one who endures to the end will be saved." Gospel of St. Matthew 5:44, 5:10, 10:22

CHAPTER 11

Friars should steer clear of women.

I command all of you not to be found in suspicious relations with women. And you may never enter the houses of nuns, except for those brothers who have permission to do so from the Holy See, as they are spiritual counselors to women. Please avoid scandal when it comes to relationships with women.

CHAPTER 12

Guidelines for going among Muslims and other nonbelievers, and final thoughts.

There will be brothers who are inspired by God to go among Muslims or other nonbelievers. They should ask permission, before doing so, from their provincial minister. Ministers should grant permission only to those who seem most prepared to do this.

Finally:

Every minister in this order must always be submissive to the Holy Pontiff, and to the cardinal of the Roman Church who has been appointed governor and protector of our simple fraternity. Ministers must remain steadfast Catholics. They must follow the holy Gospel of our Lord with all humility, and in poverty, as we have all promised to do.

No one may tamper with this Rule of ours. None among our number may oppose it. To do so is to offend God himself, and his blessed apostles St. Peter and St. Paul.

LETTER TO BROTHER ANTHONY OF PADUA (1224)

DATE: 1224

GENRE: PERSONAL LETTER

Francis's concerns about book learning had become well known by this time. We just read an admonition from him on this subject in the middle of chapter 10 of "The Rule of Life of 1223."

There is a story of Francis and the young friar who wanted to own a prayer book of his own. The young man approached his spiritual master to ask the simple question: "May I have permission to own a prayer book of my own? I want to pray with it daily." "No, no, you shouldn't," Francis said, and he walked away. The young man ran after him, confused. "But why, Brother Francis, why can't I own a prayer book? I only want to pray!" Francis was saddened, perhaps a bit confused himself. Pausing for a moment, he then turned around and pointed to the young man's chest. "Here! Here should be your prayer book!" he said. And he walked away.

St. Anthony of Padua came to the Franciscans from another religious order, and already trained as a priest and theologian. Like that young friar, Anthony simply wanted to teach theology to the other friars. . . .

> Anthony, this is your Brother Francis. I send you my love and greetings. You, Anthony, are like my bishop in this religious life.
>
> I am happy that you desire to teach the beauty of theological truth to the other friars, and I hope that you will do so. However, please, Anthony, teach them always in a way that does not dampen the fire within them for prayer and devotion. Study can do this, you know.

YOU ARE ALL SWEETNESS, MY LORD

DATE: 1224

GENRE: POEM OR SONG

One of the early Franciscan texts, written to remember St. Francis, is "The Legend of the Three Companions." These companions of

Francis were three of his earliest friends: Brother Angelo, Brother Leo, and Brother Rufino. They knew Francis best because they spent the most time with him–but also because they shared his concerns. To read the The Legend of the Three Companions *today is to get the sense that the four men shared the same heart. This is confirmed by pilgrims who visit the famous Basilica in Assisi today, who, upon entering the lower level crypt where the saint is buried, discover that Angelo, Leo, and Rufino are buried in the same place. You'll see nameplates for them there under the high altar.*

Of the three companions, we know most about Leo. From many stories, it seems that Leo was Francis's closest friend, frequent confidant, and walking companion. And Leo is the only one to whom Francis wrote a personal letter. Francis did so because Leo asked for a piece of writing when he was facing some serious temptation to sin. To put this in today's terms: Leo turned to Francis for spiritual advice and encouragement—something like what we would today find in a spirituality book.

Earlier editors made it standard practice to call this text "Praises of God." Francis of course didn't title it, and I've given it a title more in keeping with Francis's message to Leo.

God, you are holy. You are the only One.
Your wonderful deeds are all around us.

You are strong. You are great.
You are the crown, the Most High, the almighty
 sovereign.
You are, holy Father, ruler of the heavens and the earth.

You are Three Persons and you are One.
You are the Lord God of all there is.

And You are so good!
You are every good! You are the highest good!

You are alive, my Lord.
You are living and faithful.
You are love, wisdom, and meekness.
You are long-suffering, comforting, and shalom.
You are my joy.
You are my happiness.
You are my strength.
You are justice.
You are the Source of whatever I need.
You are beauty.
You are strength.
You are our only needed protection.
You will defend us from harm.
You will be our courage.
In You, we find safe-keeping.
In You, we are faithful.
In You, we find eternal life,
God almighty, merciful Savior, Amen.

According to Thomas of Celano, "Francis wrote on the parchment the encouragement that Leo required, and handing it to him, said, 'Now keep this with you all the days of your life.'"

LORD BLESS YOU, LEO

DATE: 1225

GENRE: LETTER/PERSONAL NOTE

This personal note exists in autograph form from the hand of St. Francis—something that can be said only about this piece of writing and one other. In books that collect the saint's writings, this one is almost always presented together with the one just above, because they were composed on the front and back of the same small piece of parchment. You can often see it on display in Assisi even today.

At the end of his life, Francis was simply laying upon his closest friend what is known as the traditional priestly blessing in Judaism and Christianity—found verbatim in Numbers 6:24–26. He follows it with a short, personal message:

> The Lord bless you and keep you;
> The Lord make his face to shine upon you,
> and be gracious to you;
> the Lord lift up his countenance upon you,
> and give you peace.
> Brother Leo, may God bless you always.

CANTICLE OF THE CREATURES

DATE: 1225

GENRE: POEM OR SONG

Francis composed this famous "Canticle," or song, in vernacular Italian when he was nearly blind, one year before his death. These four facts are all remarkable:

- *He is singing, showing that a poem or song can be more an aid to teaching than discourse that's didactic. The earliest Franciscans sang this song to a tune, often accompanied by instruments.*
- *No religious teachers wrote in the vernacular in the early thirteenth century. The Church said that Latin was the only language suitable for religious talk. Francis ignored this.*
- *He was a poet, but he didn't stay in the ether as poets sometimes do. This song is both paradigm bending and practical.*
- *How odd it was for a nearly blind man to write so lovingly of the physical world that he can no longer see!*

Most of all, the subject matter is surprising. Here was a medieval saint finding holiness in the created world. Where had Francis learned this theology? Nowhere. This teaching is not to be found before this moment. On the topic of the created world, the theologians could have been summed up in this one line from St. Cyprian: "Even in flowers the Enemy lies hidden." Instead, Francis sets out to praise the elements and creatures all around him.

While he composed these words, Francis was living in a simple struc-

ture of some kind just outside the walls of San Damiano where St. Clare resided with her fellow Franciscan sisters. She was caring for him.

Good Lord! You are the highest, the almighty, the All
Good!
To you belong praise, the glory, honor, every blessing!

You are glorified, O God, in all your creatures,
most of all, Brother Sun.
He brings us day and he shows us the light.
He shines with splendor so radiant and fine.
O God, Brother Sun is the warmth of you for us!

You are glorified, O Lord, through Sister Moon, too,
and all the stars in the sky.
They are yours in heaven.
They sparkle clear and precious.

You are glorified through Brother Wind,
in the air and clouds, through calm breezes and stormy
weather.
You use them for the life of all your other creatures.

Glorified are you through our Sister Water.
She is what we need.
She is so humble, so quiet, and clear.

Glorified are you in fierce Brother Fire,
who gives us such light in such darkness!
Brother Fire is bright and happy, playful and bold.

You are glorified by our Mother Earth.
Through her, you sustain and keep us.
Every plant and fruit and flower and color of
yours enters our lives by Mother Earth.

The Canticle was written in stages. Those stanzas came first. Next, Francis wrote these. He turns from expressing wonder at the world around him to one of the central themes of all his teaching: the necessity of being humble, showing forgiveness, and being peaceable. Then he writes about embracing his own death, reminding his brothers that death is nothing to be feared. She is a sister.

Glorified are you, O God, whenever someone shows
forgiveness with your love, whenever someone
accepts trouble and tribulation with peace.
Blessed is everyone who lives humbly for you
Because you, O Highest, will crown their heads.

Glorified are you, O my Lord, for Sister Death
a condition that the body may not escape.
May no one ever die with sin on their hearts!
But we are blessed who die,
Finding your highest, most holy, will,
Knowing that bodily death will not harm us at all.

Glorified and blessed is the Lord, O God.
Thank him. Serve him. Show him your humility.

LISTEN, PLEASE

DATE: 1225

GENRE: POEM OR SONG

The tradition is that Francis wrote this song also while living outside San Damiano, in St. Clare's direct and indirect care. Perhaps he is comforting the women of San Damiano, not to worry about what was to come for him. But this translation shows his words also with a broader intent.

Listen please, every little one, if you have been called by God . . .
If you have come to this place from far away . . .

We can each at least live for truth . . .
We can all aspire to die as obedient daughters and sons . . .
We can keep turning away from what's worldly . . .
We can know always the Spirit instead . . .

I, little brother Francis, can only ask of you in love . . .
please discern prayerfully all that God has given . . .
If you are one who has been hurt by sickness or worry . . .
may you find the way to bear it all in peace . . .
Know that all you have endured will soon pass away . . .
and you will find yourself wearing a crown
fitted for you in heaven by
the Virgin Mary!

MY FINAL WISHES

DATE: 1225

GENRE: WILL AND TESTAMENT

What follows is extracted from St. Clare's Rule, which she was finally allowed to write for herself, and was approved by Pope Innocent IV, in 1253. That's more than a quarter century after Francis left these wishes with Clare and for her. For years, she was urged by leaders in the Church not to take on the severity of Francis's way of life for the Second Order. Also, for years, after Francis's death, there were those in Franciscan leadership who taught that Francis's severity was not necessarily the true way. See the last line, where Francis alludes to them.

I, your little brother Francis, want nothing more than to live according to the life and poverty of our Lord Jesus Christ and his holy Mother, Mary. To this, I will persevere to my final day. I beg and urge you, my sisters, holy women, to live forever in the same holy life of poverty. Keep watch over yourselves always so that you will never abandon our life, despite the teachings or advice you may hear from anyone else.

THE TESTAMENT

DATE: 1226

GENRE: WILL AND TESTAMENT

This is almost Francis's final piece of writing, most likely dictated by him to one of his brothers while he was dying. It is his Testament in the sense that we now use the word to say "final will and testament" but also in the biblical sense, as a sign or evidence of what God is doing among him and his brothers and sisters. There are some autobiographical touches here, starting with the iconic opening: "I am Brother Francis." For that reason alone, it is most valuable.

I am Brother Francis. God showed me the ways of sin beginning with the sight of lepers and how uncomfortable it made me. But then God led me among them, and I began to learn to have compassion for them, and I began to help with their troubles. Before long, what had made me so uncomfortable became instead something sweet to my soul, even to my body.

I then left living among lepers, and for a time, I waited, until I knew that it was time for me to leave the world.

God showed me also a faith in churches. He showed me how to pray simply. So, I say, "I worship you, Lord, in every church anywhere in the world. I will praise and thank you because with your cross you have saved the world."

Then God gave me a faith in priests, those of the Roman Church, so that I would never cease to follow their advice. Anywhere in the world, I would only preach if the local priest invited me to do so. To them I give all my respect and honor. I cannot even imagine sin in these men, because I see the Son of God among them so often. I am only able to see the Son of God clearly, in this corporeal world, in his holy Body and Blood, which only priests may administer. This is the one holy mystery to be honored above all others. It should be carefully kept and protected. If I ever find our Lord's holy names, or any piece of writing sitting around, I gather them and take them to a more holy place. I also feel that we must honor theologians, all who preach the holy words of God, and every minister who offers spirit and life.

Then God gave me brothers in this way of life. I wasn't shown what to do by any one person, but by God himself, who revealed to me slowly but surely the design of the Gospel. Then I wrote it all down very simply, using few words, to show the Pope, who confirmed it for me. It was clear from the beginning that any who came to join me in this life had to first give away whatever they had to the poor, and be content with nothing in this world but a tunic, lovingly patched, a cord, and pants. We must desire for nothing else. Then, the clerical brothers learned to say the Divine Office, while the lay brothers kept the Our Father. We all lived then in churches. We were simple, and we were accountable for these things and everything else to each other.

Then God showed me how to work with my hands. He gave me the desire, too, which I still have. I want every brother to have this desire for work. If there are some who do not know what work to do, let them learn, not out of a desire for money, but because every one of us should avoid laziness. If we are not paid for the work we do, no matter, we should beg alms because we are poor. God showed me how to greet people when begging alms, and otherwise: Peace and all good.

In our poverty, we should never accept gifts that are permanent. This includes churches, and any dwellings at all. We must always remember that we are pilgrims and strangers in the world. We are guests here.

God showed me to be obedient, too. Wherever we are, brothers, we shouldn't be asking for special permissions from Rome. This means no special permissions for anything at all, no matter how spiritual or beneficial it may seem. If a brother finds himself in danger where he is, or where he is going, let him flee somewhere else and do penance, seeking only God's blessing.

I will always be obedient to the minister general of this order, whoever he happens to be. I am like a tool in his hands, prepared to go wherever he tells me, and do whatever he asks me to do. I ask one thing, now: that I may always have someone with me who will help me to celebrate the Divine Office.

Every friar should feel bound, likewise, to his minister general and other guardians, and to recite the Divine Office according to the guidelines of our *Rule.* If any brother is ever found reciting a different Office, or professing to be anything but Catholic, the others should bring him before the closest minister or guardian without delay. This is a serious matter to be dealt with right away. When his minister sees him, the minister should then send him to see the protector and guardian of this order in Rome.

No brother should ever presume to change our *Rule.* May this testament of mine remind and exhort you, my brothers, that we can always observe our *Rule* with faithfulness and Catholicity. I remain your little brother Francis.

No one, not even a minister general or a custodian, may ever add or change our *Rule* and way of life. I hope you will all keep this testament together with the *Rule,* and I ask all of you, whether clergy or laypeople, never to "interpret" the chapters of the *Rule* in order to say, this is how we really should understand it. It should be understood as it is, simply, and without fuss or gloss. Observe it in your lives until the very end.

Whoever does observe to the very end, he will be blessed in heaven. I am Brother Francis, your humble servant, and I leave you with my most holy blessing.

LETTER TO LADY JACOBA

DATE: LATE SUMMER 1226

GENRE: LETTER

Francis was in great pain, from a variety of ailments, as well as treatments he'd undergone, throughout his final years. In his final weeks and months, he knew he would die. It was then that he wrote this letter to "Brother" Jacoba, a Roman woman (Lady Jacoba de Settesoli) whom he'd first met in 1209 when he and the other earliest Franciscans were seeking approval of their rule of life. She heard Francis preaching and asked him how to live for Jesus. After discovering she was married and had children, who all lived lives of prominence in Rome, he encouraged her to follow what became the Third Order, vows and spiritual practices for being Franciscan in ordinary, domestic life. From that time on Jacoba kept in contact with Francis; she housed him and other friars when visiting Rome; and Francis often referred to her with affection.

When Francis knew he would die, he wished to see her one last time. The text of this letter comes from "The Little Flowers of St. Francis," a later compilation, which is why it often is not included in collections of Francis's writings. But it reveals the simple humanness of Francis, as well as one of his important relationships. Thomas of Celano writes of Jacoba, too, saying that when she came to Francis's bedside "she wept warm tears over him, cried out, and held him in her arms, kissing him." As a testament to her importance to him, Lady Jacoba's remains were laid to rest, after her death in 1273, in the lower crypt of the Basilica in Assisi, near those of St. Francis.

To the Lady Jacoba, servant of God,
this is your Brother Francis, the poor little man you know.
Greetings in the name of Jesus!
My friend, I know from God that the end of my life is coming near, and I would love to see you one more time.
Will you please come to St. Mary of the Angels with all haste?
You might bring a shroud which the brothers could use to wrap me, and bury me.
And I would also love some of that food you used to serve in your house in Rome.

LETTER TO BROTHER LEO

DATE: SUMMER 1226

GENRE: LETTER

Some argue that this letter is not genuine, but there is enough evidence to the contrary to include it here. Again, we see the close friendship between Francis and Leo.

Peace and good health to you, Brother Leo, from your Brother Francis.

I will speak to you once more, like a mom, summarizing all that we have shared together on the road, for years, in this short note. My motherly words boil down to this, Leo: If you ever need me, simply remind yourself of my love for you. Simply look at this letter.

And remember, however you are called by God to serve him, make him happy with your life, and remain faithful to our way of life. In all its poverty and with all its blessings, do those things, Leo. Do them with gladness.

Last, you must come see me. For your sake and mine, for your soul and mine, come see me again.

Francis's Spiritual Practices

Refer back to what he wrote in "Our Simple Rule of Life" and you'll see why so many people were drawn to St. Francis: he emphasized living faithfully and truthfully over having the right doctrine. His writings spelled out most of all how to live humbly, how to stay focused on the way, and how the ways we eat, walk, talk, clothe ourselves, care for others, including those who frighten us and who are our enemies, show us to be what we are. Most radically, he showed how touching the earth and its creatures with gentleness and care puts us in touch with the holiness around us that we may not fully understand but we can reverence. With similar attention to these details in vowed religious life, in our own time, I would compare Francis to the Vietnamese Buddhist teacher Thich Nhat Hanh more than any other Christian.

Francis was a mystic who lived his mysticism with intention and passion. He was fully present and aware. He spoke less than one expects of a saint. He was a person of action and movement. Spiritual practice was paramount. He made preaching mandatory for all who joined him in his way of life, but preaching was not always done from behind a pulpit. The earliest Franciscan sermons were more like open-air discussions, encouragements, inspirations—usually while the preacher or another friar were on the road walking, beside the road begging, in hospitals caring for the ill and accompanying the dying, repairing crumbling churches, acting as intermediaries between people in trouble and people in power, and touching with tenderness the creatures and creation around them.

Francis must have known, from about the time he and his first friends walked to Rome to see the pope, that people were watching. Is this young man genuine? Is he crazy? Is that the same boy who used to dress in his father's fancy silks? Is that proud Bernardone's boy? So some of the gestures he became known for *were* dramatic. When the whole town, for instance, gathered in the piazza in front of the bishop's house to watch Francis's father demand from Francis the money he'd stolen by selling his father's fabrics and giving to the poor, what did Francis do? He could have made up with his dad in private. He could have simply apologized. But the fabrics were gone, the money given away, so Francis stripped in front of everyone and gestured grandly, saying, "Take it all back. I have only one father, now—in heaven."

After such a demonstration, it may be difficult to grasp

that Francis was an introvert. Actors, poets, and saints often are. Any given day, Francis spent far more time by himself than with others. For every hour he was in a hospital or pulpit, there were two or three when he was in a cave, out walking alone, or awake in the middle of the night. Left to himself, he preferred quiet places. Standing prayer at night under the moon. Caves where there is a near-complete absence of sound.

In the generation after his death, Franciscans who'd learned from Francis—such as the new minister general, Bonaventure—began to share a mystical outlook on life that centered on some of these contemplative practices that Francis lived more than he taught. These teachings quickly became an indelible part of the Franciscan spirit and part of its rapid growth. Bonaventure produced writings with philosophical acumen, striving to reconcile faith and reason and writing in detail about what a mystical union with God means. The Franciscans became the most powerful religious order in the world.

Teachings of Bonaventure and others like him contrasted with the simpler teachings of Francis. From what Francis said in his letter to Brother Anthony of Padua, asking him only to teach theology to the friars if he could do so without dampening their passion for spiritual practice, I suspect that Francis himself would have sat out lessons from Bonaventure. But that naïve approach didn't survive much beyond Francis's passing. The contemplation practice that became Franciscan after his death would have been too mystically intentioned for Francis, who never allowed himself or those for whom he was a spiritual director, to remain in an introverted place for long.

Bonaventure was writing brilliant books as the Franciscan minister general, and other Franciscans were teaching mental prayer and imaginative exercises. They used books of images from the life of Christ to try to develop single-mindedness and fervency for Christ. This was accomplished by reflecting often and passionately on the words in the Gospel, as well as on pictures of the scenes in those stories. To ponder Gospel scenes, to pray with them, to imaginatively place oneself beside Christ in Gethsemane, on the Road to Emmaus, and so on, was taught as a way toward becoming changed like Christ. "Do you believe that the Blessed Francis would have attained such abundance of virtue and such illuminated knowledge of the Scriptures and such subtle experience of the deception of the enemy and of vices if not by familiar conversation with and contemplation of his Lord Jesus?" the classic text of this teaching says. Its anonymous late-thirteenth-century author then points to Francis's stigmata, saying to those who will practice this contemplation, "Thus you see to what a high level the contemplation of the life of the merciful Jesus Christ may lead."[1] Beautiful and profound as these teachings were, anyone who studies Francis's life can notice the difference between this approach and the approach taken by the saint himself. Francis never taught others to do this sort of mystical contemplation. It would have all been too bookish, too theoretical, too stuck in the imagination, for him.

Francis stood at a turning point in late medieval culture between illiteracy and growing attention to learning and books. He was on the side of illiteracy, which we easily misunderstand. Centuries of destroying the cultures of native peoples on every continent, in favor of bringing them "civilization," haven't yet shown us what we have lost from their preliterate ways of being in the world. "Reading, like speech, is an ancient, preliterate craft," writes cultural historian Robert Bringhurst. Then he offers examples of how native people, before Western civilization, were careful readers of animal tracks, bodies, and behaviors; of the speeches of birds and the movement of seas and winds; and "in infinite detail, the voices, faces, gestures, coughs and postures of other human beings. This is a serious kind of reading," he says.[2] I think he's correct, and I think this is a component of Francis's life essential to knowing him and to attempting to learn from him. Francis was focused on this kind of knowing: the kind that doesn't come in books. He liked wild things and always appreciated their wildness. He traveled seas and talked with fish. He is the saint who told birds to sing—sing!—because they can. We can't all sing. Most of what Francis knew of the Bible came from hearing Scripture read aloud and memorizing it, taking it to heart—not from studying what's in books. This also explains his love for dance and poetry—people from preliterate cultures often combined those two arts in performances rich with meaning. After Francis's death came the transition throughout Europe from this oral culture to a literate one.

• • •

There is a story that, early in his conversion, Francis was still under the power of the father who'd taught him to stay away from sick people, poor people, or anyone unfamiliar. Men and women suffering from leprosy were chief among these. They were not to be touched. One day, a leper stopped Francis on his horse and asked him for bread. Francis handed him a coin and rode away. But while he was on the road with the leper behind him, Francis experienced what Christian spirituality might call the conviction of the Holy Spirit. He knew that his actions, and his heart, were not right. Francis spun the horse around and returned to the spot where the leper still stood. Francis jumped off the horse and embraced the man, and from that moment on there was no turning back.

A heart can change, and a heart can steer the mind and the body. After that experience with the horse and the leper, Francis was always telling people to pray, and then after prayer, to go out and practice the Gospel with others. He knew from experience how willpower relates to the Spirit at work in a heart. He knew that practice—with hands and feet—is not only appropriate but necessary. Every person is in one stage of conversion or another, and the degree to which we progress depends on God's grace and our cooperation.

Seeking the Vulnerable

Seeking the vulnerable is where Francis's spiritual practice begins, because this is where spirituality functioned in his life like that jolt of electricity to a dead battery. I am referring to the time in his early twenties when he was beginning to pray and question inherited assumptions but not yet exposing himself to the lives of others. His heart was still mostly that secular, worldly, hardened heart. He'd experienced a time of brokenness: defeat, depression, humiliation (our hearts need pain in order to become healthy muscles), and the Spirit was at work on him.

Then came his encounter with the leper on the road, described earlier. Jean Vanier, the founder of L'Arche communities, where people with disabilities who have been rejected by their families and by society live together with people without mental and physical handicaps, has often said: "Love is to reveal the beauty of another person to themselves." This is what Francis did—first, simultaneously, by God's grace, that day on the road in 1205, and then, again and again, as an intentional spiritual practice.

He speaks of that first occasion in the opening words of his "Testament" (see earlier). This is the most defining paragraph in all his writings. Francis is telling how God found him when he says that it was entirely through the vulnerable. Sin, grace, mercy, and love are summarized when Francis explains:

> I am Brother Francis. God showed me the ways of sin beginning with the sight of lepers and how uncomfortable it made me. But then God led me among them, and I began to learn to have compassion for them, and I began to help with their troubles. Before long, what had made me so un-

comfortable became instead something sweet to my soul, even to my body.

He spent the next two decades trying to show his brothers and sisters how to do this, too.

Blessing Animals, Stones, Fish, Sun, and Moon

Sophisticated experts in St. Francis often miss why it was so radical that he addressed animals, stones, fish, the sun, and the moon directly. Theologians seem to skip right past the most important elementary quality about this: Francis was showing that his spiritual life—that Christian spirituality itself—begins in the world around us.

Before Francis invented the friar, to contrast the monk, vowed religious life was about being shut up in cloisters, apart from the world. Those cloisters were tightly controlled in the sense that someone living inside of one rarely went outdoors. All the action of life, including and especially what was considered religious life, took place inside. Monks prayed in choir in rooms made of stone and wood. They sometimes worked each day for short periods of time outdoors, but the most important aspects of life took place in rooms of gray and brown. Imagine the colors that were missing from such a life. Wheat fields with oranges and reds. The chromatic displays of flowers! Francis saw something much larger. He was, to use the words of an earlier mystic, Meister Eckhart, one who did not simply understand, seeing things separated from each other, but moved beyond understanding by seeing the connections—what Eckhart called the "All in all." For these reasons, Francis went about blessing every form of creation, even those that might seem to us inanimate (e.g., stones). Not only did he preach to birds—pointedly, for the first time, when human beings wouldn't listen to him—but it is even said he talked with trees. One day he called to an almond tree, "Brother Almond, tell me about God!" and the almond tree opened its blossoms. Francis insisted that gardens the friars planted must always include a strip at one end for what others, then, saw as useless: flowers. He remembered that Jesus compared faith to the glories of the lilies of the field. He must have also known, simply from observation, that flowers bring birds and butterflies and bees, and all this activity to him was joyous. It's in that context we hear him blessing and singing about Brother Wolf, Sister Fish, Brother Sun, and Sister Moon.

Holy Foolishness

Francis rolled in the snow and in rosebushes to shake off physical temptation. He traveled to various towns shabbily dressed and looking foolish, precisely to teach a lesson about simplicity and how from simplicity can come joy. He preached in his underwear before crowds when doing so was a method of teaching him and others humility. He argued with robbers, encouraging them to take even more from him than what they'd come for. He was a court jester—a jongleur, entertainer—for the spiritual life, showing with his jesting that those in power are fooling only themselves if they believe it will last. And surely the spiritual adventures one has by following a mysterious God are more interesting and vital than living the mundane ways of the world.

He also eschewed the parts of life that most of us embrace as our best opportunities for happiness: spouses, children, ownership of things, positions of authority, recognition from peers, promotions and advancement, homemaking. These are also the same things that sometimes bring us the greatest disappointment and unhappiness in life, so perhaps Francis and those like him knew what they were doing. Members of Franciscan Third Order groups have, since St. Francis first established them, been all about finding the right balance between these worlds. For Francis, at least, his spouse was Christ, his children were his spiritual brothers, authority was worth nothing in heaven, and his home was under the stars.

Denial and Dance

How odd it is that the same man who lived so ascetically at times also sang and danced and spoke of wanting to not just preach to people but also entertain them. But on closer inspection, this isn't that strange. Song and dance and thinking little of death go hand in hand. For Francis (and he certainly wasn't the first or the only such saint), the answer to living fully came by first cheating death of any hold it might have on him. By dying to what the world wants and values, he had come alive. Nothing that really matters could be taken from him anymore.

He refused to own anything. He deliberately at times ate food that others wouldn't touch for fear of sickness. He slept very little and often insisted on sleeping uncomfortably. He would stand all night in prayer. Was all this necessary? Is the person who eats less likely to be more spiritually attuned than the one who eats lavishly? It is impolite to say so, in our twenty-first century, but yes.

Our natural state is covered over with comforts, entertainments, illusions. We need a jolt we can apply to ourselves. I am told that, in a zendo, the Zen master is likely to hit you with a stick if you begin to nod off during your sitting meditation. For a Christian, and for Francis, asceticisms like fasting, dangerous actions, and intentional discomforts are not exactly that stick, self-applied, but they are ways of stripping away the things that cover up who we really are.

In all the ways that he denied himself, Francis showed himself to be from the tradition of hermits. These are practices he inherited from others. They are practices that probably need reviving today. "Self-control is, in a way, not control at all: it is the melting away of the need for certain forms of comfort and distraction. It is an *embrace* of simplicity," one cultural historian recently said in the context of responding to climate change by making significant changes in one's way of life.[3] You could say that Francis consciously changed his way of life over and over. He became conscious of needs and responded. The ancient hermit in the desert in Egypt and Syria, like Francis, like anyone today who is trying to respond personally to the needs around them, focuses on self-control.

This sort of denial and dance was then, as it is now, a way of consciously creating something—and doing something—new.

Finding Joy

This is where life is most simple: the desire we all have to be happy. Ask anyone what they want in life and they'll respond with a variety of answers, but then ask, *Why those things?* Eventually, they all boil down to: *That's what will make me most happy.* Hopefully, we get it right—where and how we pursue happiness.

Francis's spiritual practice was clear on this point, emphasizing there are many ways that the world confuses us about what it is that leads to happiness. We think we're happy, and we're not. Hopefully, we realize our mistake before it's too late.

Joy is not exactly happiness. Where happiness tends to come and go, joy lives deeper inside us. Joy is not a feeling or a posture. Feelings can be instructive, but they also change easily. Joy wells up from that deep-down place. My favorite story of all the stories of Francis is this one about joy.

Francis and Leo were walking from Assisi to a nearby town. Leo was tired. Perhaps they'd been walking a long time. Francis was upbeat and feeling good. Then it began to rain steadily. Leo started to grumble. There was no place for cover, and Francis seemed unperturbed. Then Francis said to Leo, "Do you know what perfect joy is, Leo?" "Not really," Leo said, unhappily, and in a way that was designed to discourage further conversation. They walked on a bit farther as Leo picked up his pace, walking in front of his friend, anxious to get to wherever they were going as quickly as possible. Several minutes go by, and Francis says, this time shouting up ahead to Leo, "Leo, what is joy?" This time, Leo doesn't even respond but let's out a sort of growl. *Enough of this,* he thinks to himself. *I'm not interested in a lesson right now.* Again, minutes go by, the rain is falling even harder, and Francis repeats the question again. Leo spins around and yells back, "I don't know! What *is* perfect joy?!" Francis replies, "If, when we arrive, we're wet down to the bones, and shivering from cold, hungry as can be, and we knock on the door to signal our arrival, and a friar opens it but doesn't recognize us, and slams it shut in our faces, fearful that we've come to rob him, and we're left standing in this rain even longer, and then perhaps we knock again and someone else opens the door and hits us with sticks, yelling at us like strangers or robbers, if we remain patient and humble and loving, even then, through all of that, well, that, Leo, reveals the source of perfect joy."

That is salvation.

Final Thoughts

One of the holy early Franciscans was a man called Thomas. Thomas was Francis's exact contemporary, born in the hill-top town of Celano in central Italy. He came to know Francis in about 1215, when Thomas took up the life of a friar. A poet and scholar, Thomas would go on to write three books about Francis, and he would do many of the investigations that led to Francis's beatification and canonization after his death. Thomas also wrote a biography of St. Clare.

In the opening paragraph of book two of Thomas's *Life of St. Francis,* having spent book one on the years 1206–24 (from the time of Francis first hearing God speak to him in San Damiano to his imagining the Incarnation in the Greccio live Nativity), Thomas refers to those eighteen years as a time of "ongoing conversion." He tells us that this was an innovation–not an innovation of Thomas in how to talk about someone in a religious biography, but Francis's unique way of understanding the meaning and purpose of the religious life: as continual conversion.

This is why I have often used the language of "early in his conversion," "after his conversion," et cetera, when talking about Francis throughout this little book. The word "conversion" in English comes from a root that means "turned around." That's how Francis understood it and how Thomas of Celano relayed his understanding whenever he wrote about his friend. That "turning around" took place during a particular period of time; Francis could point to it and say, *That's where I started to turn around.* But he always understood that he had to remain turned around or keep turning around, meaning turning away from the dominant, overriding, and alluring concerns of the world around him. It isn't that the world is an illusion—it is very real, and if we spend our days being lured by it our lives can become an illusion. This is how the late Eugene Peterson put it: "The puzzle is why so many people live badly. Not so wickedly, but so inanely. . . . There is little to admire and less to imitate in the people who are prominent in our culture. . . . People, aimless and bored, amuse themselves with trivia and trash. Neither the adventure of goodness nor the pursuit of righteousness gets headlines."[1]

That's what the way of life meant for Francis, and that's still what it means.

Notes

Introduction

1. Dario Fo, *Holy Jester: The Saint Francis Fables,* trans. Mario Pirovano (Tuxedo Park, NY: Opus, 2018), ix.
2. Dario Fo, *Plays: 1* (London: Methuen Drama, 1997), 1.
3. Dario Fo, *Holy Jester,* ix.
4. Milton T. Walsh, in *Ludolph of Saxony: The Life of Jesus Christ, Part One, Vol. 1, Chapters 1–40* (Collegeville, MN: Cistercian Publications, 2018), xxvii.
5. Jean Francois Godet-Calogeras, "Francis and Clare and the Emergence of the Second Order," in *The Cambridge Companion to Francis of Assisi*, ed. Michael J. P. Robson (New York: Cambridge University Press, 2012), 115.
6. Claude Lévi-Strauss, in *Lévi-Strauss: A Biography,* by Emmanuelle Loyer, trans. Ninon Vinsonneau and Jonathan Magidoff (Medford, MA: Polity, 2018), 1.

Francis's Teachings

1. Andrew Schelling, *Tracks Along the Left Coast: Jaime de Angulo and Pacific Coast Culture* (Berkeley, CA: Counterpoint, 2018), xxiv.

Francis's Spiritual Practices

1. *Meditations on the Life of Christ: An Illustrated Manuscript of the Fourteenth Century,* trans. Isa Ragusa, eds. Isa Ragusa and Rosalie B. Green (Princeton: Princeton University Press, 1961), 1, 3. Though this classic was once attributed to St. Bonaventure, we now know the author is anonymous.
2. Robert Bringhurst, *A Story as Sharp as a Knife: The Classical Haida Mythtellers and Their World,* 2nd ed. (Madeira Park, BC: Douglas & McIntyre, 2011), 14.
3. In *Learning to Die: Wisdom in the Age of Climate Crisis,* by Robert Bringhurst and Jan Zwicky (Saskatchewan: University of Regina Press, 2018), 56.

Final Thoughts

1. Eugene Peterson, *Run with the Horses: The Quest for Life at Its Best* (Downers Grove, IL: InterVarsity Press, 2009), 14.

If You Want to Read More

Recommended Biographies of Francis

Green, J. *God's Fool: The Life and Times of Francis of Assisi.* Translated by Peter Heinegg. New York: Harper & Row, 1987.

Manselli, R. *Saint Francis of Assisi.* Chicago: Franciscan Herald Press, 1984.

Sabatier, P. *The Road to Assisi: The Essential Biography of Saint Francis.* Jon M. Sweeney, ed. Brewster, MA: Paraclete Press, 2014.

Thompson, A. *Francis of Assisi: The Life.* Ithaca, NY: Cornell University Press, 2013.

Vauchez, A. *Francis of Assisi: The Life and Afterlife of a Medieval Saint.* Translated by Michael F. Cusato. New Haven: Yale University Press, 2012.

Recommended Popular Editions of the Writings of Francis

Sweeney, J. M., trans. and ed. *The Complete Francis of Assisi: His Life, the Complete Writings, and* The Little Flowers. Brewster, MA: Paraclete Press, 2015.

———, trans. and ed. *Francis of Assisi in His Own Words: The Essential Writings,* 2nd edition. Brewster, MA: Paraclete Press, 2018.

Recommended Scholarly Editions of the Writings and Early Franciscan Documents

Armstrong, R. J., J. A. Wayne Hellmann, and W. J. Short, eds. *Francis of Assisi: Early Documents.* Vol. 1, *The Saint.* New York: New City Press, 1999.

———, eds. *Francis of Assisi: Early Documents.* Vol. 2, *The Founder.* New York: New City Press, 2000.

———, eds. *Francis of Assisi: Early Documents.* Vol. 3, *The Prophet.* New York: New City Press, 2002.

Habig, M. A., ed. *St. Francis of Assisi: Writings and Early Biographies; English Omnibus of the Sources for the Life of St. Francis,* 4th edition. Chicago: Franciscan Herald Press, 1983.

Francis and Animals

Armstrong, R. J., et al., eds. "The Assisi Compilation," in *Francis of Assisi: Early Documents,* Vol. 2: *The Founder.* New York: New City Press, 2000.

Ugolino, Brother, comp. *The Little Flowers of Saint Francis.* Introduced and rendered in contemporary English by Jon M. Sweeney. Brewster, MA: Paraclete Press, 2016.

Francis and the Church

Boff, L. *Saint Francis of Assisi: A Model for Human Liberation.* Translated by John W. Diercksmeier. Maryknoll, NY: Orbis Books, 2006.

Whalen, B. E. *The Medieval Papacy.* New York: Palgrave Macmillan, 2014.

Francis, the Crusades, and Islam

Guibert of Nogent. *Monodies* and *On the Relics of Saints: The Autobiography and a Manifesto of a French Monk from the Time of the Crusades.* Translated by Joseph McAlhany and Jay Rubenstein. New York: Penguin Books, 2011.

Moses, P. *The Saint and the Sultan: The Crusades, Islam, and Francis of Assisi's Mission of Peace.* New York: Doubleday Religion, 2009.

Parrinder, G. *Jesus in the Qur'an*. New York: Oxford University Press, 1977.

Francis and Foolishness

Fo, D. *Holy Jester: The Saint Francis Fables.* Translated by Mario Pirovano. Tuxedo Park, NY: Opus Books, 2017.

Paintner, C. V. *Illuminating the Way: Embracing the Way of Monks and Mystics,* Chap. 1. Notre Dame, IN: Sorin Books, 2016.

Sweeney, J. M. *The St. Francis Holy Fool Prayer Book*. Brewster, MA: Paraclete Press, 2017.

Francis and Poverty

Agamben, G. *The Highest Poverty: Monastic Rules and Form-of-Life.* Translated by Adam Kotsko. Stanford, CA: Stanford University Press, 2013.

Senocak, N. *The Poor and the Perfect: The Rise of Learning in the Franciscan Order, 1209–1310.* Ithaca, NY: Cornell University Press, 2012.

Francis and Spirituality

Bodo, M., OFM. *Francis: The Journey and the Dream.* Cincinnati: Franciscan Media, 2012.

Cunningham, L. S. *Francis of Assisi: Performing the Gospel Life.* Grand Rapids, MI: Eerdmans, 2004.

Sweeney, J. M. *The St. Clare Prayer Book: Listening for God's Leading.* Brewster, MA: Paraclete Press, 2007.

———. *The St. Francis Prayer Book: A Guide to Deepen Your Spiritual Life.* Brewster, MA: Paraclete Press, 2004.

Unamuno, M. de. *Our Lord Don Quixote.* Bollingen Series. Princeton: Princeton University Press, 1967.

Acknowledgments

Many thanks to Joel Fotinos, for the invitation to write this book for the St. Martin's Essential Wisdom Library. It has been a pleasure to participate in such a project. Thank you, also, to Gwen Hawkes, editor, and all the fine team at St. Martin's Publishing Group, for their excellence in carrying this book into the light.

St. Francis is dedicated to Adam Bucko, a soul friend. We met when the writing was first under way, and our conversations, and your friendship, have inspired and challenged me. Thank you.

About the Author

Maury Woll

JON M. SWEENEY is an independent scholar and a respected writer. A biographer of St. Francis and translator of his writings, Sweeney's books on Franciscan subjects have sold 200,000 copies. He's the author of more than thirty books, including *The Pope Who Quit,* which was optioned by HBO. Sweeney is editor in chief and publisher of Paraclete Press. He's appeared on *CBS Saturday Morning* and numerous other programs. Jon is married to Rabbi Michal Woll, is the father of four, and lives in Milwaukee.

THE ESSENTIAL WISDOM LIBRARY

Sacred Texts for Modern Readers

January 2020

July 2020